Page 1: The spectacular F[...]
their Gnat trainers.
Previous pages: The Fairey *Swordfish*, a World War II
bomber and torpedo-carrier.
Left: A McDonnell Douglas A-4N Skyhawk II light
attack aircraft.

ave '. . . around the spinning world the magic golden girdle of flight.'

CONTENTS

Below: Although we now know that Bartolomeu de Gusmão flew the first model hot-air balloon, it was Joseph and Etienne Montgolfier who were first to create a full-size man-carrying balloon of this type. The illustration depicts the ascent of a Montgolfier balloon at Lyon in January 1784.

Right: But balloon flight was not powered flight. Could the balloon help to hasten progress from one to the other? Jacob Degen, a Swiss clockmaker who lived in Vienna, thought that it could and built this strange device with which he flew: but of course it was the balloon and not Degen's fantastic efforts that provided the lift.

Below right: Unfortunately, balloons went in the direction dictated by the prevailing wind. If a balloon could be given some kind of power plant then it could be steered: leading, logically, to the airship. The first almost-practical example was built by Renard and Krebs in France in 1884, but long before that the more imaginative than practical had produced designs like the one illustrated here.

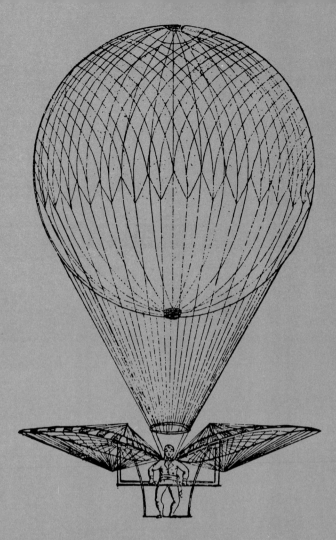

THE STORY OF **AIRCRAFT**

SEVEN DECADES OF POWERED FLIGHT
THE STORY OF AIRCRAFT

DAVID CHARLES

For Captain James Bowman BEA, a close and valued friend who, to borrow words from Ethel B. De Lasky, has hel

First published 1974 by
Octopus Books Limited
59 Grosvenor Street, London W1

ISBN 0 7064 0364 9

© Octopus Books Limited

Produced by
Mandarin Publishers Limited
14 Westlands Road,
Quarry Bay, Hong Kong

Printed in Hong Kong

BEFORE THE FIRST DECADE

*it is our duty not to rest until we have
attained to a perfect scientific conception
of the problem of flight.*
Otto Lilienthal

Menacing in appearance, the all-black aircraft stands ready for flight. Through the windshield its pilot can see a ribbon of concrete stretching, seemingly, to infinity: a man-made 'philosopher's stone' to transmute the inert mass of metal into a bird of the air.

The note of its engines rises to the scream of a banshee, tongues of flame blasting from the jet-pipes as, brakes released, it begins to move forward.

In the cockpit, the pilot unleashes more power, selecting partial reheat. Care is needed: too much thrust at this stage could rip the tyres from their rims, but as the machine streaks down the runway a sudden thump confirms full reheat as jet-pipes become pinpointed by shock-cones.

Rotation: that moment when a miracle occurs, as man's metal bird lifts into the air. Up comes the nose and the big delta-winged aircraft climbs effortlessly – already flying faster than the maximum speed of World War II fighters.

Almost before the pilot has time to report his take-off the machine has passed the 60,000 ft (18,300 m) level and is still climbing: navigation lights are retracted to prevent them from being burned away by exposure to the slipstream. Then, at about 70,000 ft (21,300 m), the machine is levelled off for cruising flight. The pilot, encased in a Gemini-type space-suit, complete with 'goldfish-bowl' helmet, can sit and work in comparative comfort, despite the fact that some parts of the airframe of his machine are already heated to more than 1,000 degrees Fahrenheit (583 °C).

Science fiction? No. A brief description of a routine take-off of one of the USAF's SR-71A reconnaissance aircraft. It has a counterpart on the other side of the Iron Curtain, the Mikoyan MiG-25, and these two reconnaissance machines were the world's fastest front-line aeroplanes in 1973.

They have a direct link with aircraft of 60 years earlier, for the first military aeroplanes were required only to fulfil a reconnaissance role. Little more than a decade after the first powered flight in 1903, man had already put the aeroplane into warlike operation. By that war's end, when the 'stick-and-string' birds had already learned to spit death, Orville Wright was to comment: 'What a dream it was; what a nightmare it has become.'

But we have still a long way to travel back in time if we would seek the beginning of this dream: as far, perhaps, as a thousand years before the birth of Christ when, in ancient China, an unknown man held in his hand the string of the world's first kite. As it traced its unsteady pattern of flight against the canopy of the heavens, its happy inventor might have imagined that, one day, he might be able to commune with his honourable ancestors without first having to cross the Valley of Death.

Let us, then, follow this fascinating story of men who by sacrifice and endeavour have conquered the airlanes of the world, have travelled weightlessly in space and, as we have seen, have walked on the moon.

In taking an objective look at the history of aviation we must dispense with myth and legend and stick to the hard facts. But having said that, we must also be prepared to accept some early inventions as fact, even though it is impossible to label them with a precise date. For example, there is no doubt that the Chinese were building and flying kites about 1000 BC, and their man-flying kites were undoubtedly the first man-carrying aircraft. Unfortunately, we have no accurate dates.

Between 100 and 300 AD the Romans adopted dragon-like standards, hollow tubes of cloth, each supported at the head by a metal ring which served also to form the mouth, and into which the wind could blow to inflate and move the body. The metal ring was mounted on a pole for the standard-bearer and, as he moved forward on foot or horseback, his 'dragon' behaved rather like the well-known windsock. It is suggested that not only did the standards strike fear into the hearts of the enemy; they had a practical application, allowing archers to judge the strength and direction of the wind.

The windsock banner (*draco*) developed gradually, in kite form, into a frightening psychological weapon, devised to belch fire and smoke. In fact, it is recorded that at the battle of Wahlstatt in 1241, the Tartar army unfurled an immense draco, from which '... poured forth vile-smelling steam, smoke and fumes, which engulfed the whole Polish army.'

Below: The Australian Lawrence Hargrave added an important contribution to aviation history by invention of the box-kite. Many early successful powered aircraft were to utilize construction of this type.

Right: Invention of the practical hydrogen balloon by Professor Charles soon led to rapid advancement of the sport of ballooning. The picture re-creates the Victorian atmosphere of a balloon meet at the Crystal Palace in London.

Kites were all very well, but they flew only when tied to a string. To ambitious men who dreamed of flying as freely as the birds they seemed a dead end. How ironic that no one thought seriously about the factors that made a kite fly: why some did and others did not; why a long tail was sometimes needed to give the kite stability. How close they were to elementary gliding flight.

But would-be aviators were preoccupied by the birds who managed to fly without being attached to a string. They were not static objects, but became airborne by flapping their wings: it was reasonable to assume that if man wanted to fly he would have to copy their technique.

Leonardo da Vinci (1452–1519) was the first scientist to study the problems of flight, but he was obsessed with the need to copy the flapping wings of the bird. He was convinced that man's muscular power, enhanced by mechanical principles involving levers, was adequate to achieve flight. In his studies of the birds he failed to appreciate the significance of the gliding and soaring flight of the gulls, achieved with outstretched, unmoving wings. He was not to know that the bird's lightweight structure is launched into the air by a remarkable powerhouse of pectoral muscles, which can account for as much as 15 per cent of the total bodyweight. A specially evolved four-chamber heart, beating at speeds of up to 1,000 beats a minute in some species, provides fuel for these muscles via an oxygen-enriched bloodstream.

Man was not so adapted; instead he had an enquiring mind. One of those who evolved an original idea was Francesco de Lana-Terzi, a Jesuit priest, who in 1670 designed a lighter-than-air craft suspended from four copper globes. He planned to evacuate the air from the globes which, being lighter than the volume of air they had displaced, would float aloft away into the blue. He

overlooked the fact that if they were light enough to do this, they would collapse as a result of atmospheric pressure.

At any rate, de Lana-Terzi was sufficiently farsighted to appreciate the military applications of his flying-machine, commenting: '... iron weights could be hurled down to wreck the ships and kill their crews; or the ships could be set on fire by fireballs and bombs. Not only ships, but houses, fortresses and cities could thus be destroyed...' The air power versus naval power controversy is seen to have originated nearly two-and-a-half centuries before powered flight became reality.

Over a century after da Vinci's death, Giovanni Alfonso Borelli (1608–79) came to the conclusion, after a most detailed study of bird flight, that man's muscular structure was inadequate for him to get himself airborne, commenting: 'It is impossible that men should be able to fly craftily by their own strength.' It was sufficiently authoritative to bring an end to heavier-than-air flight experiments until the 19th century.

Six years after Borelli's death, Maria Alvares Lourenco gave birth to a son at Santos, in the Portuguese province of São Paulo, Brazil. Named Bartolomeu, he later changed his surname to Gusmão in acknowledgement of the education provided by a benefactor, Father Alexandre Gusmão.

As a student at Coimbra University, Portugal, Bartolomeu de Gusmão, as he was by then known, began the design of an 'aerostatic' machine under the patronage of King John V of Portugal. Simultaneously, he designed a hot-air balloon, demonstrating this successfully before King John, Queen Maria Anna and other dignitaries on 8 August 1709. He thus pre-dated the Montgolfier brothers by 64 years.

Aviation history has, until quite recently, credited the Montgolfiers with the invention of the hot-air balloon. Now the facts have been put right, but this in no way lessens the achievement of these two Frenchmen.

On 5 June 1783 at Annonay, France, their first balloon, 38 ft (11.5 m) in diameter and a composite structure of linen panels and paper lining, was released after being charged with hot air over a fire of wool and straw. When the restraining ropes were released, it climbed majestically to a height of more than 6,000 ft (1,830 m).

Four months later, on 15 October, an even larger *Montgolfière*, restrained by 85 ft (26 m) tethering ropes and with a wicker basket suspended beneath it, carried the first man into the air. The fearless aeronaut was a young physician, Jean-François Pilâtre de Rozier, who commented afterwards to the inevitable newshounds that he had suffered: '... no giddiness, no incommoding motion, no shock whatever'.

In the following month he made a free flight, ranging for some $5\frac{1}{2}$ miles (8.8 km), with the Marquis d'Arlandes as passenger/stoker. The latter's task was to refuel with straw the brazier that maintained the supply of hot air, as well as to damp down any potential fires when sparks caused the balloon's envelope to smoulder.

Just over six weeks later, on 1 December, Professor J.A.C. Charles and Marie-Noel Robert made a completely successful two-hour flight in a hydrogen balloon, marking the beginning of a sport that was to sweep across the world.

Man was airborne at last, but there was a snag–he could not travel where he wished but must be satisfied with the wind's direction. John Selden (1584–1654) had already devised navigational equipment: 'Take a straw and throw it up in the air, you shall see by that which way the wind is.'

Straws in the wind might serve for sport or amusement; there were still men who wanted to fly like the birds, purposefully and with direction. It was not until almost 70 years later that, on 24 September 1852, Henri Giffard piloted a full-size steam-powered airship from Paris to Trappes in France. This was a somewhat marginal and fortuitous

Right: Percy Pilcher's 'Hawk' glider of 1896, seen after the fabric had been restored in 1964.
Above right: In America, Octave Chanute designed goodlooking hang-gliders with the aid of a young engineer, A.M. Herring.
Far right: Dr S.P. Langley, Secretary of the Smithsonian Institution, was regarded as favourite for the race to achieve manned, powered flight in a heavier-than-air craft after his steam-powered 14 ft (4.27 m) span model had flown for $\frac{3}{4}$ mile in 1896. Here is his full size *Aerodrome* aboard its houseboat launcher on 7 October 1903.

performance: it was the electrically powered airship *La France*, built by Charles Renard and Arthus Krebs, which demonstrated for the first time on 9 August 1884 a lighter-than-air craft that could be steered on a chosen course, irrespective of the wind.

While these lighter-than-air *divertissements* had been taking place, the true pioneers of aviation had been making some real progress. Most significant was the work of Sir George Cayley (1773–1857), a Yorkshire baronet, who was the first man to understand the potential of the kite–the 'wing' that had been a toy for centuries. His first model glider, built in 1804, was little more than a kite mounted with positive incidence on a stick. At the other end of the stick was an adjustable cruciform tail to control the direction of flight.

This model was capable of stable gliding flight, and within five years he had built a scaled-up version that could carry a small boy as passenger. By then he could already see the way ahead, commenting: 'I feel perfectly confident, however, that this noble art will soon be brought home to man's convenience, and that we shall be able to transport ourselves and our families, and their goods and chattels, more securely by air than by water, and with a velocity of from 20 to 100 miles per hour.'

By 1853, when Cayley was 80 years of age, he had constructed a full-size triplane glider which carried his volubly protesting coachman in flight across a small valley. This was, indeed, a great achievement. But behind the achievement was the first clear understanding of the aerodynamic theory of flight. A treasured possession of London's Science Museum is a silver disc, engraved by Cayley in 1799. One side bears a diagram delineating the forces of lift, drag and thrust. Little wonder that he was to become known as the 'Father of Aerial Navigation'.

In the footsteps of Cayley followed men like William Samuel Henson (1805–68), Félix du Temple (1823–90), Alexander Mozhaisky (1825–90) and Clement Ader (1841–1925). All struggled to achieve flight with aircraft powered by completely inadequate engines.

Contemporary with these men was the German Otto Lilienthal (1848–96). His book *Der Vogelflug als Grundlage der Fliegkunst* (Bird Flight as the Basis of Aviation) is a classic, describing the way in which a bird drives itself through the air by a propeller-like motion of the outer primary feathers. He was quite convinced that true powered flight would be achieved by ornithopters (flapping wing aircraft), but realized that he must get 'on intimate terms with the wind', to use his words, as the first stage in developing a powered aircraft.

To gain this 'intimacy' he built his first fixed-wing glider in 1889. Neither that, nor the one which followed, were successful. The third proved that he was on the right track,

Left: Langley's full-size 'Aerodrome' failed to achieve success and left the field open for the Wright brothers. With their No.3 glider, which sported a rudder, they made hundreds of successful piloted gliding flights.

Below: The Wrights' next move was to build a larger, powered version of the No.3 glider. There was little data on wing sections, so they built their own wind tunnel. This replica is in the Smithsonian Institution.

but it was his *Normal-Segelapparat* (standard flying machine) of 1894 that enabled him to make repeated controlled glides of more than 1,100 ft (335 m).

All his machines were hang-gliders, meaning the pilot hung by his arms below the machine and by contortions of his body could achieve limited control in all three movements pitch, roll and yaw. Lilienthal was to die when one of his gliders stalled and side-slipped into the ground, breaking his spine. He survived until the following day, 10 August 1896. His tombstone bears the epitaph *Opfer müssen gebracht werden* (sacrifices must be made). Lilienthal's death was a great loss to aviation, but he had tabulated his progress meticulously, so that others could benefit from his work.

Percy Pilcher, in Britain, had visited Lilienthal in Germany. He had watched him fly, talked with him, and had even been allowed to try his hand on some of the gliders. Unfortunately, he too was to die following an accident similar to Lilienthal's, on 2 October 1899.

Of the glider pioneers, only Octave Chanute in America was left; being in the right place at the right time, he was able to help enthuse the Wright brothers in their efforts to achieve powered flight.

Orville and Wilbur Wright, bicycle builders of Dayton, Ohio, began by constructing a biplane kite in 1899. Its direction of flight could be controlled by wires that allowed

them to twist (warp) its wings in flight. When it proved successful, they built a glider of 17 ft (5.18 m) wing span which, flown mainly as a kite at Kill Devil Hills, near Kitty Hawk, North Carolina, revealed some unexpected aerodynamic snags. Glider No.2, flown in 1901, had increased wing area, but did not resolve all of their problems. Thus, the winter of 1901/2 was spent largely in testing some 200 wing sections in a wind tunnel of their own design and construction.

Glider No.3, flown in 1902, benefited from the winter spent in aerodynamic research. Sporting a rudder, it spanned 32 ft (9.78 m), had a wing area of 305 sq ft (28.34 m²) and weighed 116.5 lb (48.3 kg) without the pilot. They discovered very quickly that their hard work during the winter nights had not been wasted: No.3 was to make hundreds of successful gliding flights.

Well satisfied with progress they returned home and began construction of what became known as the *Flyer*. This was somewhat larger than the No.3 glider, with a wing span of 40 ft 4 in. (12.29 m), length of 21 ft 1 in. (6.43 m), wing area of 510 sq ft (47.38 m²) and empty weight of 605 lb (274.4 kg). But if they had solved the aerodynamic problems, there still existed the number one headache that was worrying would-be aviators around the world: provision of a suitable power plant for the machine.

After tentative enquiries had shown there was no suitable

Right: A rarely-seen photograph of the Wright 'Flyer' on the starting track at Kill Devil Hill, prior to the trial on 14 December 1903. The four men were from the Kill Devil Hill Life Saving Station, and had helped the brothers to move the machine to the launching site, but the two small boys ran away in fear when its engine was started.

Below right: The triumphs of 17 December 1903 ended, the *Flyer* stands with its forward elevators damaged. Clearly seen is the chain drive for the two hand-carved pusher propellers.

engine available they characteristically decided to design and build their own. This emerged as a four-cylinder, water-cooled, in-line engine, developing from 12-16 hp. Mounted between the wings it had to drive via chains two contrarotating pusher propellers, which were mounted on extension shafts to bring them aft of the trailing-edge of the wings.

The Wrights did not have, or know how best to make, suitable propellers. Once again it was a matter of study and experiment before the laminated spruce propellers could be made and fitted to their shafts.

At the beginning of December 1903 the *Flyer* was conveyed to Kitty Hawk and, after erection and preparation, a first attempt at flight was made on Monday 14 December, a bright, cold day with moderate wind. The engine was started. Wilbur was at the controls and, as the little machine accelerated, Orville, who was steadying a wingtip, lost his balance. The *Flyer* climbed, stalled, and crashed almost before one could take breath.

Two days of repairs followed and on the miserably cold, windy morning of 17 December the *Flyer* was prepared again. The five witnesses/helpers could hardly believe their eyes when, with Orville at the controls, it took to the air, to record a first flight of 12 seconds, covering a distance of about 120 ft (36.60 m).

A total of four flights were made that day, the last piloted by Wilbur. Orville described how:

'Wilbur started the fourth and last flight at just twelve o'clock. The first few hundred feet were up and down, as before, but by the time three hundred feet had been covered the machine was under much better control. The course for the next four or five hundred feet had but little undulation. However, when out about eight hundred feet the machine began pitching again, and in one of its darts downwards, struck the ground. The distance over the ground was measured and found to be 852 ft; the time of the flight 59 seconds...'

Despite the odds, despite the challenge posed by Britain's Hiram Maxim, Germany's Karl Jatho and their own countryman, Samuel Pierpont Langley, determination had carried the Wright brothers to success.

Man's ambition was realized at last. He could fly like the birds—just!

Right: The Wright brothers had achieved the first almost-controlled flight in a powered heavier-than-air craft, yet it was Santos-Dumont in this ugly-looking No. 14 *bis* who gained the acclaim.

Below: The Frenchman who deserved his financial reward and hero's welcome for the first Channel crossing was Louis Blériot, photographed alongside the Type XI monoplane after 'landing' at Dover on 25 July 1907.

FLEDGLINGS
1904·13

mighty things from small beginnings grow
John Dryden

At 4.30 we could see all around. Daylight had come. M.le Blanc endeavoured to see the coast of England, but could not. A light breeze from the south-west was blowing. The air was clear. Everything was prepared. I was dressed as I am at this moment, a khaki jacket lined with wool for warmth over my tweed clothes and beneath my engineer's suit of blue overalls. My close-fitting cap was fastened over my head and ears. I had neither eaten nor drunk anything since I rose. My thoughts were only upon the flight and my determination to accomplish it this morning.

'4.35! Tout est prêt!' Le Blanc gives the signal and in an instant I am in the air, my engine making 1,200 revolutions – almost its highest speed – in order that I may get quickly over the telegraph wires along the edge of the cliff. As soon as I am over the cliff, I reduce my speed. There is now no need to force the engine.

The words are those of the Frenchman, Louis Blériot, recorded in the *Daily Mail* after he had made the first successful crossing of the English Channel, on 25 July 1909, to win the prize of £1,000 offered by that newspaper for such an achievement.

It had been something of an adventure, for indifferent visibility and lack of a compass meant there was little hope of an accurate landfall. There was also the problem of the 22/25 hp Anzani engine which, prior to that date, had demonstrated regularly a serious loss of power after only 20 minutes of flight. Blériot reckoned he might need a non-stop run of around 40 minutes!

Inevitably, as expected, the engine began to show signs of failure in mid-Channel, beginning to run roughly as it became overheated. Blériot held his breath as the little monoplane edged closer and closer to the sea. Then came the miracle of a sudden, sharp shower, the raindrops sizzling on and cooling the exposed cylinders. As the note of the engine steadied, it began to develop more power.

But now he was in a world of swirling mist and light rain, visibility gone. Let Blériot take up the story again: 'I can see nothing at all. For ten minutes I am lost. It is a strange position, to be alone, unguided, without compass, in the air over the middle of the Channel...And then, twenty minutes after I have left the French coast, I see the cliffs of Dover, the castle, and away to the west the spot where I had intended to land. What can I do? It is evident that the wind

has taken me out of my course... Now indeed I am in difficulties, for the wind here by the cliffs is much stronger, and my speed is reduced as I fight against it... I see an opening in the cliff...I cannot resist the opportunity of making a landing on this green spot...I enter the opening and find myself again over dry land. Avoiding the red buildings on my right, I attempt a landing, but the wind catches me. I stop my motor and the machine falls.'

Blériot was safe and sound on the grassy slope of North Fall Meadow, almost in the shadow of Dover Castle. A mere 37 minutes had been necessary to complete the flight from Les Baraques, near Calais, but they were minutes that quickly brought realization of what might one day be accomplished by the aeroplane. No longer would seas and navies offer guarantee of isolation and security.

In spite of what had been accomplished by the Wright brothers, French aircraft then held a leading position in world aviation. This ascendancy had begun on a cold October day in 1906 when, late in the afternoon, a strange-looking machine known as the No.14 *bis*, built and piloted by Santos-Dumont, a Chaplinesque, diminutive Brazilian, had made a rather tentative flight of just under 200 ft (61 m) from the Bois de Boulogne, Paris.

Witnessed by about a thousand people, photographed and officially timed, it was hailed as the world's first flight by a powered heavier-than-air craft.

How was this possible when the Wright brothers had made the first flight nearly three years earlier? It can be explained by three facts. The first was a garbled and incredulous story filed by a freelance reporter, which made American news editors shy away from publishing what they regarded as science fiction. Secondly, the Wrights were not really publicity-minded, and wanted to get on with the business of developing a really reliable aircraft. Finally, when they did stage a press demonstration, in May 1904, the *Flyer* went shy and the best they could offer the newshounds was a 60 ft (18 m) glide. Not surprisingly, the press boys believed that the claims made for and by the Wrights were just so much talk. This was truly ironic, especially because 5 October 1905, slightly more than a year before, the 'first' flight made by Alberto Santos-Dumont, the Wright's

Above: The model of Félix du Temple's full-size powered aeroplane forms part of the Qantas collection. During 1874 the original aircraft recorded the world's first powered take-off, down a ramp, followed by a brief 'hop'.

Right: Also from the Qantas collection is this model of a Lilienthal glider. During 1890–6, in aircraft of this type, Lilienthal proved the practicability of heavier-than-air craft.

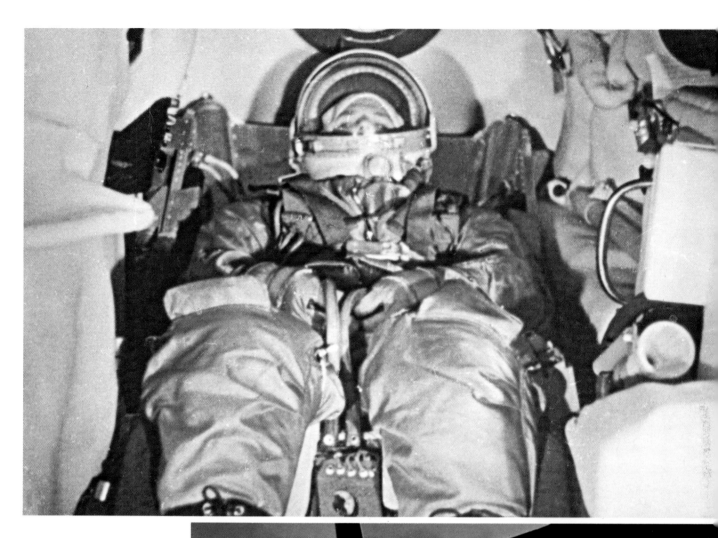

Above: Inspired by pioneers like Lilienthal, the Wright brothers achieved true powered flight at the end of 1903. Within a man's life-span we have now reached out far beyond the dreams of the pioneers. Russia's Major Yuri Gagarin, seen here in the spacecraft Vostok 1, was the first man to travel in orbit around the earth.

Right: Russia's Luna 9 spacecraft recorded the first soft-landing on the lunar soil.

Right: In England, A.V. Roe had been the first national to fly an all-British aeroplane when his frail Roe I Triplane made a 100 ft (30 m) powered flight on 13 July 1909. The illustration shows a replica built for the film *Those Magnificent Men in their Flying Machines.*

Far right: In the first early days the aeroplane was intended as a sporting vehicle. Here Henry Farman, flying the type of biplane used by Grahame-White in 1910, makes a graceful turn around a pylon.

Below right: Grahame-White was also to demonstrate his skill in America, and is seen here landing between the White House and State War and Navy Building in Washington, D.C.

No.3 *Flyer* had completed a non-stop flight that exceeded 24 miles (39 km).

But all French attempts to produce a really practical aeroplane had met with little success by the end of 1907. Fresh impetus was added to their efforts in the latter half of 1908, when Wilbur Wright arrived in France to demonstrate the new Model A. His initial flight was made before a highly sceptical audience, but they were shocked into silence when they saw the graceful and controlled flight of the Wright machine.

Lack of progress was not then confined to France. The same held good for all countries, where pioneer builder/pilots were trying their utmost to construct an aeroplane that would, as a bonus to the sheer joy of creation, also bring fame and fortune.

Perhaps the biggest problem was the very inadequate power plants then available. Most had derived from the growing motor car industry, but these were heavy, water-cooled engines. The air-cooled engine was a far better proposition, dispensing with the parasitic weight of radiator, pipes and water. But this meant a change in shape, to a radial configuration, each of the cylinders being in the air-flow.

The snag was that low-powered engines meant low forward speeds, and low-forward speeds were inadequate to cool sufficiently the overloaded, overheating engine, even when the cylinders were exposed to the airstream.

Early aviation owes a considerable debt to Laurent Seguin of France who, together with his brother, made a serious effort to overcome the problem. Their solution was the rotary engine, in which propeller, cylinders and crankcase turned as one rather frightening chunk of metal, the crankshaft being fixed to the airframe. The flywheel inertia of this mass provided smooth running, even at low throttle openings and the cylinders, windmilling in the slipstream, were prevented from overheating.

Their first five-cylinder engine of 1908 developed one horsepower for each 3.3 lb (1.4 kg) of its weight, at a time when contemporary engines weighed about 6 lb (2.7 kg) per horsepower. Soon there was a range of these Gnome power plants, as they were called, and once the pioneer builders became accustomed to the odd sight of a whole engine spinning round, they began to use them to such an extent that they dominated the aviation scene. On the debit side they were rather noisy, and it was often said they consumed more oil than petrol. This was not strictly true; nonetheless, airframes and pilots gradually became permeated with castor oil.

It had been assumed that better power plants would solve all the problems of the airframe builders. They were to find this manifestly untrue and had to begin a slow process of improving their part of the whole.

We still refer to aircraft of that period as being of 'stick-and-string' construction. This is rather unkind, and certainly inaccurate. Beautifully made mahogany frames reflected the skill of the cabinet maker; hand-wrought metal fittings, lovingly fashioned hand-carved propellers and a high standard of finish give the lie to this rather derogatory phrase. It

Above: The Apollo moon-landing missions ended with No. 17 in 1973. They had carried 12 men to walk on lunar soil, leaving behind three of these Boeing Lunar Rover vehicles which had made the last three missions highly successful.

Right: First men to land on the moon were Neil Armstrong and Edwin Aldrin of the United States. The general public soon lost interest in routine moon landings, and scenes like this astronaut setting up an experiment near to the lunar module.

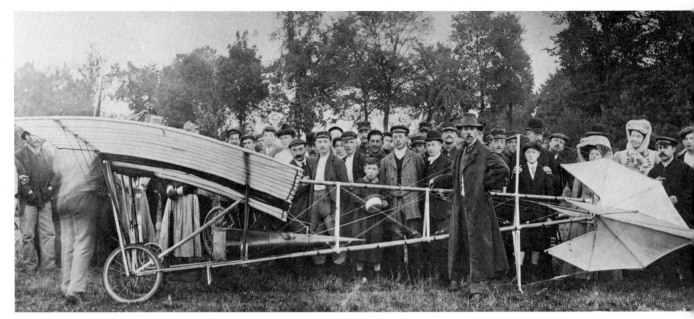

Above: Perhaps one of the earliest designs intended for the homebuilder was that of the little *Demoiselle*, built by Santos-Dumont. He had overlooked the fact that while it could lift a man of his small stature into the air, it was unable to leave the ground carrying more normal-sized constructors.

is not intended to be derogatory; rather does it imply the hit-and-miss design and construction of that era.

The real problem was lack of knowledge of aerodynamics. Efficient wing sections had still to be developed, and cantilever construction techniques were needed to eradicate the multiplicity of struts, king-posts and bracing wires that held the whole structure together.

French aviation was the driving power: in America nobody was seriously interested, and in Britain red tape was still holding up development. One of the first real eyeopeners was the Rheims aviation week—*La Grande Semaine d'Aviation de la Champagne*—held on the plain of Bétheny, near Rheims, from 22 to 29 August 1909.

Vast crowds of enthusiastic spectators thrilled to this new spectacle, the roar of engines, the all-pervading smell of castor oil and the new favourites who, day after day, gave breathtaking displays of skill in their 'flying machines'. By the time it had ended Henry Farman had flown one of his biplanes for an incredible 112 miles (180 km), Louis Blériot held the speed record at almost 48 mph (76.95 km/h), and Hubert Latham had coaxed an Antoinette VII monoplane to a height of 508 ft (155 m). Such performances, reported throughout the world, demonstrated that the aeroplane had become a practical vehicle.

Early in the following year another Frenchman, Henri Fabre, made the world's first take-off from water in a powered hydro-aeroplane. An odd-looking machine of his own design, it covered a distance of about 1,500 ft (457 m) at Martigues, near Marseilles. American and British machines

Right: One of the most graceful of the early French monoplanes was the *Antoinette*, designed and built by Leon Levavasseur. A version is seen taking part in a flying meeting.

Below: S.F. Cody's entry for the first British Military Aeroplane Competition held at Larkhill, Salisbury Plain, in August 1912. Although it won the competition, it is clear that it was a dead-end design.

Top left: A replica of the famous Curtiss JN-4, a World War I trainer and post-war mount of the barnstormers. It originated at the close of this decade (1904–13) when Glenn Curtis employed one of the Avro engineers to design a tractor biplane for him. It was to remain in United States military service until 1927.

Left: Replica of the Bristol 'Box-kite' built by the British & Colonial Aeroplane Company Ltd at Bristol in 1910. In effect it was little more than a copy of a Henry Farman biplane, with detail improvements, slightly differing examples being powered by Grégoire, E.N.V., Gnome and Renault engines of from 50 to 70 hp.

Above: Typical of the scout aircraft which equipped United States Air Service squadrons when they entered World War I is this replica of a Nieuport 28C-1. It even bears on its fuselage the 'Hat-in-the-Ring' insignia of the famous 94th Pursuit Squadron.

Above: Daring young
ladies were prepared to
risk their lives in the
wonderful flying machine.
Claude Grahame-White
and passenger provide a
charming picture of the
pioneering days.

Right: The first Interna-
tional Air Race at Hendon
in 1913 was won by
Claude Grahame-White.
He is seen here flying
across the winning line.

were soon to follow suit but, unlike Fabre's aircraft which had been designed specifically as a water-borne craft, theirs were adaptations of landplanes, with floats replacing the wheeled landing gear.

The year 1910 was memorable also for the introduction of the world's first regular but unscheduled air passenger services, provided by the German airships *Hansa*, *Sachsen*, *Schwaben* and *Viktoria Luise*. Operated by *Deutsche Luftschiffahrts A.G. Direktion*, known more usually as Delag, they carried some 34,000 passengers without serious accident before World War I brought an end to their operations.

At this stage in the development of aviation, Germany was certainly in the lead so far as investment in aeronautical research was concerned. To such an extent that, as the 1914–18 war began to loom on the horizon, statesmen of other European nations expressed their very considerable concern at the lack of progress in what could clearly become an important weapon of war.

But the lack of effort to militarize the aeroplane was not really surprising. Wars had always been fought by land armies locked in mortal combat; there were few dyed-in-the-wool staff planners who had any reason to suppose that the next war would be any different. Who wanted noisy, temperamental aeroplanes that could be flown only when the weather was clear and calm? It was just possible that they might serve for reconnaissance or as despatch carriers. Inevitably, early military trials were intended to find out whether they were capable of even such menial tasks.

Individuals of some nations could see beyond their noses. In America, Eugene Ely flew a Curtiss biplane off an 83 ft

(25 m) platform built over the fore deck of the cruiser USS *Birmingham*. This event, suggesting the potential of an aircraft carrier, took place on 14 November 1910. On 18 January 1911 he did even better, landing on and taking off from the cruiser USS *Pennsylvania*, which was 13 miles (21 km) offshore.

In Britain a significant biplane took to the air for the first time on 1 April 1911. This was A.V. Roe's Type D biplane the prototype of which, with some engine modifications to increase power and floats replacing the wheel landing gear, recorded the first take-off from water for a British aircraft. More significantly, the Type D was the progenitor of the Avro 504 which first flew in 1913, one of the most valued training aircraft of the British Royal Flying Corps (RFC). It was to remain in service with the Royal Air Force (RAF) into the late 1920s.

Following early development of airships in Germany, British politicians at last began to realize their military potential, and money was made available for the provision of aeroplanes. It was not before time. Prior to that the British Army had acquired a Balloon Section, as a unit of the Royal Engineers. It also had man-flying kites, provided by an American citizen, Samuel Franklin Cody, who was appointed Chief Instructor in Kiting in 1906.

But Cody's vision extended beyond kites and string, however big, and he fitted a small engine to one of his kites so that he could fly it unpiloted. When it worked, he began construction of a full-size aircraft, which led to the big bamboo-and-canvas biplane which made the first officially-recognized flight of a powered aircraft in Britain, on

Above: To celebrate the 50th anniversary of the first non-stop flight over the North Atlantic, this superb replica of the Vickers Vimy was built. This shot shows the colourful drama of that never-to-be-forgotten take-off from St John's, Newfoundland.

Above right: Famous for its association with German ace Manfred von Richthofen, the Fokker Dr I triplane was used almost exclusively by him after his first flight in one of the type in September 1917.

Right: A replica of a German Pfalz D XII, a single-seat fighter; powered in its original form by a 160 hp Mercedes in-line water-cooled engine, it was a formidable opponent in the closing stages of the war.

Below: Most of the early machines were built by rule-of-thumb: science had not then invaded this territory. Stressing tests for the wings of this Co-anda monoplane are clearly practical rather than theoretical.

Right: As early as 1911 the classic biplane was beginning to take shape. This Avro Type D, the original version with transverse radiator and a 35 hp Green liquid-cooled engine, was the progenitor of the famous Avro 504.

16 October 1908. It became known officially as British Army Aeroplane No.1.

Cody's machine was a dead-end design, but following some further reduction of the opposition to aeroplanes, the Balloon Section was allowed to 'afford opportunities for aeroplaning'. Soon after this the balloon factory at Farnborough acquired a young designer named Geoffrey de Havilland who, working in conjunction with F.M. Green, 'reconstructed' a crashed Voisin biplane. Rather more than a repair, the Voisin emerged finally as a new machine, designated B.E.1. It gave valuable service until written off in a crash in early 1915.

The B.E.1 showed advanced aerodynamic and structural thought, and was described subsequently by Sir Walter Raleigh as: 'The first machine of its type, it (became) the revered grandfather of the whole brood of factory aeroplanes.' When the British Royal Flying Corps was established, on 13 April 1912, the B.E.1 was numbered among its first aircraft.

France, too, was concerned about airship development in Germany, and increased her aircraft production. Germany, who had been preoccupied with airships, suddenly realized that it had neglected aeroplanes and began to hurry their design, construction and the establishment of military flying schools.

But perhaps the most startling aeroplane had taken shape in Russia. There, Igor Sikorsky, later to gain international fame and a niche in history for development of the world's first practical single-rotor helicopter, had built an enormous four-engined aircraft known as the *Grand*.

With a wing span of 92 ft (28.00 m) and powered by four 100 hp Argus water-cooled engines, it was flown by Sikorsky for the first time on 13 May 1913. Just under three months later the *Grand*, which was easily the world's biggest heavier-than-air craft at that time, made a 1 hr 54 min. non-stop flight with a pilot and seven passengers on board.

There was no doubt that the skill of aircraft designers and builders was increasing. As 1913 closed, a trio of Frenchmen held the speed, distance and height records. Prévost, flying a Deperdussin monoplane, had flown at 126.67 mph (203.86 km/h); Seguin in a Henry Farman biplane had covered 634.54 miles (1,021.2 km) in a closed circuit; and Georges Legagneux had climbed his Nieuport monoplane to a height of 20,079 ft (6,120 m).

Earlier in the same year, on 16 April 1913, the first contest for the Schneider Trophy had been held at Monaco. It had attracted little attention, being one item on the long programme of the Monaco Hydro-Aeroplane Meeting. It was won by Prévost, flying a Deperdussin monoplane equipped with floats. No man then living could have guessed that aircraft developed to win this trophy would change the face of history in the World War II.

In fact, he could hardly have expected there would be a second World War when the first had not yet started. But the war clouds were already gathering over Europe. Those with aviation leanings might well have pondered how the fledgling aircraft would fit into the cut and thrust of the war that seemed inevitable.

WAR & PEACE 1914-23

Right: An outstanding
single-seat fighter of
World War I was the
Royal Aircraft Factory
S.E.5a designed mainly by
H.P. Folland. British 'ace'
Major 'Mick' Mannock,
scored more than 50 of his
73 confirmed victories in
this type of machine.

Below: One of the immor-
tal aircraft of early British
aviation is the Avro 504,
an outstanding two-seat
trainer which was used
until the late 1920s.

*chronicle the wars
of kites and crows fighting in the air*
John Milton

No sooner had the engine stopped than it must have gone stone cold owing to the small amount of water in the jackets, though steam was coming out of the radiator relief pipe quite merrily for some little time. This fact we had not realized until quite low down I opened the throttle and got no response whatever.

I then shouted to Grieve to get busy on the petrol pump, and he was very soon bending forward and pumping hard enough to push the carburettor needle valves right off their seats and flooding the jets with petrol.

But nothing happened at all except that the Atlantic rose up to meet us at rather an alarming rate. We were gliding down wind at a pretty good speed, the sea was very rough, and when we hit it I knew very well that there was going to be a crash of sorts, and that if he remained where he was Grieve would probably get badly damaged, as he would be shot forward head first on to the petrol tank. So I clumped him hard on the back and yelled to him that I was going to 'land'.

We were then about 10 feet above the particularly uninviting-looking waves.

And then we had the biggest stroke of luck.

Thanks to Grieve's pumping the engine at last fired, I gave her a good mouthful of throttle, she roared away with the best will in the world, the dive flattened and tilted into a climb and we were soon back again at a four-figured altitude and very glad to be there.
So wrote Harry G. Hawker in his book *Our Atlantic Attempt*, published in 1919, describing how he and Lt. Cdr. Macken-

zie Grieve, RN, tried to accomplish the first west-east crossing of the North Altantic.

Taking off from St.John's, Newfoundland, on 18 May 1919, they had soon found the single engine of their specially-built Sopwith *Atlantic* biplane was overheating. Hawker assumed there was a blockage—probably sediment—in the cooling system and that this might be dispersed by stopping the engine, diving 2,000 or 3,000 feet and then restarting it.

At the first attempt it had seemed to work, but the words which open this chapter describe the near-disaster of a later endeavour to overcome the problem that was gradually boiling away the entire contents of the cooling system.

Eventually the moment came when it was impossible to keep the machine in the air any longer. Almost miraculously they sighted a vessel, the Danish steamship *Mary*. After ditching the *Atlantic* alongside they were rescued; but on both sides of the ocean it was believed they had perished in their attempt to span the unfriendly ocean. The Danish vessel had no radio, and it was not until a week later that the world was to learn of their providential rescue.

This would suggest that aviation had made considerable progress since the end of 1913, when a Channel crossing was still an adventure. Then, not even the most foolhardy would have considered it possible to cover the forbidding waters of the Atlantic Ocean. In fact, the pilots of the

Right: Igor Sikorsky, the Russian pioneer who was later to earn fame as the designer of the world's first practical single-rotor helicopter, was responsible also for the *Ilya Mouriametz*. This was the world's first four-engined bomber to see active service, followed by the German R-Type 'giants'.

Below right: When Captain Murray Sueter of Air Department of the British Admiralty demanded a 'bloody paralyser' of an aeroplane for strategic bombing attacks on targets in Germany, Handley Page designed and built an 0/100, which led eventually to the V/1500. A four-engined bomber with a wing span of 126 ft (38.40 m), it was the largest aeroplane built in Britain until that time, but the war ended before it entered service.

RFC.'s Nos. 2, 3, 4, and 5 Squadrons, who flew their aircraft to France at the beginning of World War I, were aware they had set out on something of an adventure. Each had an inflated inner tube from a motor car tyre round his waist in case they had to come down in the Channel. Fortunately the tubes were not needed.

But the question then uppermost in the military mind was whether or not the sporty boys' new-fangled machine could give any useful service in the still-conventional land battles. It did not take long to find that the answer was a very positive 'yes'. Field officers of both sides realized quickly the vital reconnaissance role of the aeroplane, as well as its ability to spot for, and direct the fire of, artillery batteries.

So much so, that it soon became necessary to find ways of preventing the reconnaissance machines of the enemy from having access to airspace. Initially, this was quite a sporting affair, pilots and observers from both sides being armed with revolvers or rifles with which they took pot shots at each other. In the main this was humorous rather than injurious: more positive means of destruction were needed.

Thus developed the whole family of military aircraft: armed reconnaissance machines, armed escorts for their protection, fighters to attack both, bombers to blast the bases from which they operated. But in the early days of the war this was far in the future.

It was obvious that escorts or fighters would need to carry machine-guns to attack the enemy; but where to mount them? If the gun was to be aimed and fired by the pilot it needed to be mounted on the upper fuselage. Only a few shots from such a gun would quickly bring about his destruction as the bullets chewed their way through the propeller. So most of the early fighters were two-seaters, the gunner being sited forward in the fuselage nose and the engine mounted behind the wings, driving a 'pusher' propeller.

Unfortunately, such aircraft were usually too slow to catch their prey, and the French had the idea of attaching steel deflector strips to the aft side of the blades of a 'tractor' propeller. A machine-gun was mounted on the fuselage upper surface and fired through the propeller disc: if a bullet hit a blade it was prevented from damaging it by the deflector strip.

On 1 April 1915, the French pilot Roland Garros took his Morane-Saulnier monoplane into action, equipped with forward-firing machine-gun and propeller-blade deflectors. In a head-on attack, his German adversary went spinning to destruction without knowing what hit him. But after only five victories with this 'revolutionary' weapon, Garros force-landed on the wrong side of the line and the secret was out.

There is no reason to suppose that German designers were ignorant of the value of a gun that could fire harmlessly through the propeller disc. The discovery of the French device, crude though it was, meant that their

Left: Most famous of the German fighter/scout aircraft of World War I was the Fokker D VII. It was so successful in combat that, in fact, it became singled out as one of the items which *had* to be handed over to the Allies at the Armistice.

Below: Not quite so well-known, but a favourite of the German 'ace' Ernst Udet, was the Pfalz D XII fighter which became active in August 1918. Illustrated is the last known airworthy example.

Right: Although the Vickers Vimy flown by Alcock and Browne achieved the first non-stop west-east crossing of the North Atlantic, it was the British airship R.34 which made the first double crossing, shown here as it came in to land at Mineola, Long Island, on 6 July 1919.

machines must have a similar capability to maintain parity. Some of Germany's best aircraft had been evolved by the Dutch pioneer, Anthony Fokker, and he was asked to copy the French idea. He chose, however, to solve the problem in a very different way, designing an ingenious mechanism to 'interrupt' the discharge of a round of ammunition from the machine-gun if a propeller blade was in the line of fire.

As soon as his agile monoplane fighters had been fitted with the new interrupter gear, they began to take a heavy toll of Allied machines. Their ascendancy became known as the 'Fokker scourge', lasting from October 1915 until April 1916, when Allied fighters began to hit back with forward-firing guns. They were not then fitted with interrupter gun gear, but the British had improved D.H.2s and F.E.2Bs of 'pusher' configuration, while the French Nieuport biplane carried its gun on top of the upper wing so that its line of fire cleared the propeller disc.

To offset the advantage held by the Germans during the period of the 'Fokker scourge', allied aircraft designers had done their utmost to improve speed and manoeuvrability of their fighters. When they, in turn, were equipped with interrupter mechanism and forward-firing guns, the boot was on the other foot.

This was very much the pattern of air fighting for the remainder of the war. First one side, then the other, would have temporary superiority as new aircarft and weapons were introduced.

Initially, Germany had seemed to hold the advantage so far as strategic bombing was concerned, her Zeppelin airships having the necessary range to strike at the British homeland. They were soon to discover their vulnerability to tempestuous weather and the enemy's improving fighter aircraft. As a result, the German developed their 'giant' bombers: the twin-engined Gothas and the Zeppelin Staaken R series.

The latter were the most revolutionary aircraft built by the Germans during the war, the R. VI being powered by four engines and having a wing span of nearly 139 ft (42.36 m). Although slow (only about 84 mph:135 km/h) they had an endurance of seven to ten hours, according to load. The first of these to attack London, on the night of 17/18 February 1918, scored a direct hit on St. Pancras railway station. But it was the daylight attacks on London, made by the Gothas in June and July 1917, that caused a major outcry.

So great was the rumpus that the British Government was forced to transfer fighter squadrons from France to provide a home defence force. It was only an interim measure: General J.C. Smuts was given the task of investigating the whole structure of the British air forces. When his findings were put into report form, in August 1917, he recommended establishment of an Air Ministry and amalgamation of the RFC and Royal Naval Service (RNAS). In due course was born the child of this union: the Royal Air Force, on 1 April 1918. Maj. Gen. Sir Hugh Trenchard was its first Chief of the Air Staff.

Until the German attacks on London, Allied bombing had been almost entirely of a tactical nature, in direct support of land operations. Now there was a call for retaliation, and Handley Page O/100s began to drop their loads of up to 16 112 lb bombs on targets in the German homeland. To make these attacks more effective an improved version of the Handley Page bomber was put into production, the O/400, and the design of new, larger strategic bombers was initiated, leading to development of the Handley Page V/1500 and Vickers Vimy. But before the last two machines were ready for operational service, the 'war to end wars' was over.

Many people believe that the pressure of this new war in the air speeded the transition of the aeroplane from a rather unreliable sporting vehicle into a fast, robust and trustworthy machine. This is far from true. The most significant advance had been in the design and construction of aero-engines that were far more powerful and reliable. It was fortunate that this was so, for they had the task of dragging through the sky airframes which, in the main, had grown in size and weight with the availability of more powerful engines and had undergone little aerodynamic refinement.

There were some exceptions, chiefly in Germany, where stressed-skin wooden structures had been developed, and Hugo Junkers was busy evolving steadily improving all-

Above: With the war's end, there were several contenders for the £10,000 *Daily Mail* prize for the first North Atlantic non-stop crossing. Among them was Freddy Raynham and Captain W. Morgan with the Martinsyde *Raymor*, seen here as they crashed on take-off from Newfoundland.

Left: Growing carrying capability, range and reliability of aircraft left little doubt that civil aviation services would develop quickly after the war's end. The first regular scheduled international air services between Britain and the Continent were initiated by George Holt Thomas' Aircraft Transport and Travel Ltd on 25 August 1919.

Air transport provided adventure, with a capital A. This lovely photograph of a D.H.9 of Aircraft Transport & Travel Ltd on charter to the Dutch airline KLM, shows how passengers were clad for their ordeal.

Above: Shipowners S. Instone & Co. Ltd began a Cardiff-London-Paris air service to provide fast transit for the company's staff and documents. They soon began to offer public services, and this picture shows the Instone brothers photographed in front of the company's Vickers Vimy G-EASI *City of London*.

metal monoplane aircraft. It is no exaggeration to state that the cantilever low-wing monoplane configuration developed by Junkers was ultimately to have a profound effect on civil and military aircraft of the future.

But the war was over. Now men could turn to the pursuits of peace and the introduction of world-wide travel over the skylanes. That had been the dream of the pioneers: the moment had arrived to make the dream reality.

It was not to prove as easy as had been expected. Ordinary men and women still believed that flying was not for them. Certainly it was no substitute for the tried and trusted car, ship and train and, if all reports were true, it was far more expensive. The enthusiasts were those who had flown military aircraft throughout the four years of war. They could appreciate the benefits that air travel could offer, and if the public would not come to them, they would have to set out to convince men and women everywhere that the aeroplane had much to offer.

But there were men of vision who, long before the war ended, had begun to make plans for civil air services. The first of these to begin operations after the war was the German, *Deutsche Luft Reederei*, who, on 5 February 1919, inaugurated a 120 mile (193 km) route from Berlin to Weimar. Britain's Air Transport & Travel Ltd, founded by George Holt Thomas, despatched its first D.H.4A 'passenger airliner' to Paris on 25 August 1919. A solitary and bold man named George Stevenson-Reece was Britain's first passenger on the first-ever daily international service. He paid £21 (nearly $50) for the privilege of a far from luxurious cross-Channel flight. That sum of money, in 1973 currency, would carry him in luxury across the Atlantic.

Aviation meetings became commonplace in the attempts to popularize the aeroplane as a means of transport. Stunt flying and wing-walking showed that aircraft were becoming more reliable; they were thrilling spectacles, but induced few people to take to the air. A five-shilling 'flip' in the front cockpit of a war surplus biplane; the wind in your face; its song through the bracing wires on landing approach: these were the true ingredients of the drug which became an addiction for growing numbers of enthusiasts.

But it needed more spectacular achievement to convert the public *en masse*. Lord Northcliffe, founder of the *Daily Mail*, had been an early believer in the aeroplane's potential. Prizes offered by that newspaper had done much to stimulate early progress. The offer of a £10,000 prize for a first Atlantic crossing had put Harry Hawker and his companion in the situation mentioned at the beginning of this chapter, and only a month later the prize was won.

On 14/15 June 1919, flying what was more or less a standard Vickers Vimy, Capt. John Alcock and Lt. Arthur Whitten-Brown made the first non-stop crossing of the North Atlantic. Taking off from St. John's, Newfoundland, they completed the 1,890 mile (3,042 km) flight to Clifden, Ireland, in 16 hr 27 min. Before the end of the same year the Australian brothers, Keith and Ross Smith, had taken off from Hounslow airfield and reached Darwin, Australia, in just under 28 days. Their 11,130 mile (17,912 km) journey had occupied 135 hr 55 min of flying time.

Clearly, the aeroplane was becoming capable of long distance travel, and in the following year a Vimy was used to create the first air link between England and South Africa. But these were special flights, not the day-to-day routine of scheduled passenger services. The would-be air traveller still needed to be blessed with reasonable funds of money and courage if he was to take his confined seat in a converted wartime bomber.

With no air-conditioning or heating passengers were supplied with warm flying clothing–even with hot water bottles in really cold weather. Meteorological services were non-existent, and navigational aids limited to a doubtfully reliable compass. Not surprisingly, pilots navigated by 'Bradshaw', following the railway lines that gleamed below. It was a little disconcerting, when bucking a headwind, to find themselves being easily outpaced by the cumbersome train that used those tracks.

Perhaps the most forward-looking of the early British airlines was Daimler Airways. When it initiated its London-Paris route at the beginning of April 1922 it began operations with the de Havilland D.H.34, the first specially designed airliner, which could carry nine passengers in wicker chairs. They even introduced stewards to serve refreshments to the passengers.

But the great problem as this decade neared its end was to make airline services pay. Too many companies were chasing too small a nucleus of passengers. On 1 April 1922 the British government introduced massive subsidies to enable the Daimler Airways, Handley Page Transport and The Instone Air Line to become established on a sound economic basis. But this aid had a three-year limitation and there was insufficient inducement for airline companies to make long-term plans and invest large sums of money in new aircraft, equipment, airport facilities and other service improvements.

The Hambling Committee, whose recommendations gave birth to Britain's Imperial Airways, came about in this climate. During the next decade this airline was to blaze trails across the world and establish a code of safety and service for others to follow.

Below: In Germany, Hugh Junkers was beginning to develop cantilever monoplane aircraft of all-metal construction, utilizing corrugated metal skins to carry some of the structural load. Illustrated is an F 24 serving with Deutsche Lufthansa.

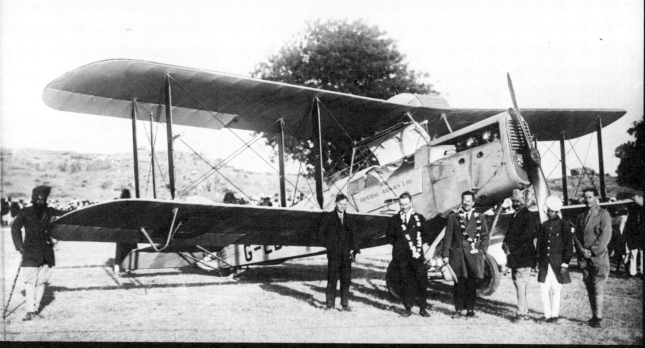

Top: Post-war civil
aviation in the United
States began with the
carriage of air mail in
ex-service American-built
de Havilland aircraft,
powered by the nationally-
designed Liberty engine.

Above: Survey flights for
the air trunk routes of
Imperial Airways were
made by Alan Cobham
(later Sir) in 1924–6. He
is seen here with the de
Havilland D.H. 50 at
Datia, India, in the com-
pany of Sir Sefton Branc-
ker and the Maharajah.

THE AEROPLANE COMES OF AGE 1924-33

forward and upward; with a steady sail;
battling his way across the furious skies –
night after night he carries on the mail;
and none will know his name, unless he dies
Naomi C. Katz

Poets are rather special people. So often they manage to distil into one brief verse a subtle permutation of words that paints a broad and colourful story. That quoted above is, of course, a generalization. It was certainly not true for the mail pilot who wrote the following words:

I open the throttle and start a climbing turn. I don't dare pull the nose up steeply. I don't dare chandelle around the hangars to celebrate my arrival, as I often do coming in with the night mail at Chicago . . .

I climb to a thousand feet. There are the camps of Paris again like a lake of stars . . . I level off for the downwind stretch. The windsock hasn't changed—still bulged and angling across the line of hangars . . .

I'm a quarter-mile downwind now—back on throttle—bank around for a final glide. Is my nose down far enough? Yes, the airspeed's at ninety miles an hour . . .

It's only a hundred yards to the hangars now—solid forms emerging from the night. I'm too high—too fast. Drop wing—left rudder—sideslip—Careful—mustn't get anywhere near the stall . . . The wheels touch gently—off again—No, I'll keep contact—Ease the stick forward . . . Slower, now—left rudder—reverse it—stick over the other way—The Spirit of St Louis swings around and stops rolling, resting on the solidness of earth, in the centre of Le Bourget.

I start to taxi back towards the floodlight and hangars—But the entire field ahead is covered with running figures!

What a great moment of aviation history, recorded by Charles A. Lindbergh in his superb book *The Spirit of St Louis*, describing in fascinating detail his thoughts and actions during the 33 hr 39 min. solo flight from New York to Paris.

This was *the* flight, the one that set the world alight. If a man could start out alone from America, in a small aircraft with only one engine, and land safely in Europe, almost a day and a half later, then the aeroplane was surely good to carry ordinary men and women on routine flights. The aeroplane had come of age.

This happened in 1924 at the beginning of the decade which was to record some significant progress. But all was not well at its start. True, the first airlines had become established: companies like Deutsche Luft Reederei, Sven-ska Lufttrafik AB, KLM and the British airlines, who founded the International Air Traffic Association (IATA) in 1919. Their problem was still to find enough passengers to make their efforts worthwhile.

In America the situation was less bright. Not only had they failed to follow up the world leadership given by the Wrights in 1903, they had not even succeeded in accelerating their aircraft industry sufficiently during World War I to put a nationally-designed combat aircraft into service on the western front.

They were not slow, however, in the post-war development of air mail services, using initially the British-designed open cockpit D.H.4. Many war surplus D.H.4s with the American-designed Liberty engine were taken over by the Post Office Department in 1919, and were soon busy speeding the mails across the vast distances of the United States. And in creating their air mail services, they began to establish a network of beacons to guide the air mail pilots by night or in bad weather. These were to prove of immense value when the first commercial airlines began to operate.

But for struggling airlines this was primarily the decade when air mail was of more importance than passengers. Not only was it available in increasing and profitable quantities, but it was an ideal cargo for the aircraft of that era. It did not mind being squeezed into any available space, was indifferent to cold or heat, and did not grow impatient at the frequent and sometimes extensive delays.

Britain's Imperial Airways similarly discovered that air mail was a profitable business, and its de Havilland D.H.66 Hercules biplanes, ordered in 1925, had plenty of space for the money-earning mail, but only seven seats for passengers. This company was nevertheless reaching out across the world. In the years 1924-26 Alan Cobham made his memorable survey flights for the British trunk routes, to India and Burma, South Africa and Australia.

Biplanes still dominated the aviation scene; civil, commercial and military. Indeed, in 1925 one of the greatest little biplanes of all time made its entrance: the two-seat Moth, designed by de Havilland. The first really practical two-seat light aeroplane, it was responsible for the development of the flying club movement throughout the world.

Above: The Ryan 'NYP' (New York–Paris) monoplane, *Spirit of St Louis*, in which Charles Lindbergh electrified the world with his solo crossing of the North Atlantic on 20/21 May 1927.

Right: *Hengist*, one of the Imperial Airways' fleet of Handley Page H.P.42s that were the 'queens' of the London-Paris route in the 1930s.

Right: In 1925 Geoffrey de Havilland's little Moth made a quiet entry, but it was soon to be heard and known affectionately all round the world, responsible more than any other aeroplane for the spread of the flying club movement.

It was so reliable that many pilots whose names are enshrined in aviation history used this little machine to set up astounding records. In it Amy Johnson made a solo flight from England to Australia, and the late Sir Francis Chichester used a Moth to brave the hazards of the Tasman Sea. His flight from Australia to New Zealand must rank as an outstanding feat of transoceanic navigation.

In the commercial field it was the Handley Page H.P.42 that is remembered with similar nostalgia. These big, stately and slow-flying aircraft, which Imperial Airways used on their London-Paris route in the 1930s, carried more passengers between Britain and the Continent than did all other airlines combined. Together the small fleet accumulated about ten million miles of flight–without harming a single passenger until the last of them disappeared during a wartime flight in 1940.

Military aircraft, in the main, held to the biplane configuration which had then almost reached the zenith of its development. The Hawker Fury of 1931 was an outstanding example of the way in which progressive evolution had produced a compact single-seat fighter. When it entered service with the Royal Air Force it was its first front-line aircraft, capable of exceeding 200 mph (322 kmh). Those who flocked to the RAF display at Hendon in 1933 were thrilled by the Furies of No 25 Squadron, which took off, performed formation aerobatics and landed, all the time linked by elastic ropes.

But the heyday of the biplane had already passed, spurred by the clean-looking monoplanes evolved for the Schneider Trophy Races, and by the pioneer work in civil airliners which had been taking place in Europe and America. European airports had already become accustomed to the sight of the Junkers Ju 52/3m, a three-engined cantilever low-wing all-metal monoplane with corrugated skins. It first entered service with the German national airline Deutsche Lufthansa in 1932, and the company eventually had no less than 230 registered in its name. On very similar lines were the Dutch Fokker and American Ford Trimotors.

Another significant development of this period was the first rotary-wing aircraft. The Spaniard Juan de la Cierva

had been working hard to discover why previous attempts to fly a single-rotor helicopter had ended in failure; why the machine canted over on its side as soon as it left the ground. Realizing it was because the advancing rotor blade created more lift than the opposite retreating blade, he designed an ingenious flapping hinge for each blade. The resulting movement of the blades, relative to each other, balanced out the lift forces and made the rotary wing a practical proposition. He did not, however, build a helicopter, but replaced the wings of a conventional aircraft with his rotary wing to create an autogyro (named by him *Autogiro*). It performed successfully, able to make very short landings, and when he arranged a mechanism so that the engine could spin up the rotor before take-off, he was able to make 'jump starts', pointing the way to the true helicopter that his flapping-hinge blade would one day make possible.

We must not overlook the fact that lighter-than-air craft have their part in history. In fact, at one period there was much debate as to whether airships, rather than aircraft, should carry passengers on the world's long-distance routes.

We have already mentioned the first non-stop Atlantic crossing by Alcock and Brown in mid-June 1919. Little over two weeks later, on 2 July 1919, the British dirigible HMA R.34 took off from East Fortune, Scotland, and after facing severe thunderstorms and headwinds landed safely at Mineola Field, Long Island, New York on 6 July. Her non-stop Atlantic flight with 31 persons on board had taken just over 108 hours. The return crossing, between 9 and 13 July, took 75 hr 3 min.

This double Atlantic crossing is seldom acclaimed with the same enthusiasm as the rather more dicey trip of Alcock and Brown. Yet the R.34 had carried 31 persons and made a safe landing at the end of each flight. Both Britain and Germany were to champion development of the airship, and the British R.101 of 1929 had an overall length of 724 ft (220.68 m) and maximum diameter of 132 ft (40.23 m).

This liner of the air was designed to carry up to 100 passengers. The main lounge was 60 ft (18.29 m) by 32 ft (9.75 m), tastefully decorated and furnished with comfortable settees and easy chairs. A 32 ft (9.75 m) by 20 ft (6.10 m)

Left: The elegant appearance of the military biplane as it approached its zenith was typified by the Hawker Fury. That illustrated is in the insignia of the *Force Aérea Portugesa*.

Below left: Look at the sleek lines of the Supermarine S.68 seaplane designed by R.J. Mitchell, which captured for Britain the Schneider Trophy. The parallel lines alongside the fuselage were cooling ducts for the lubricating oil of the Rolls-Royce 'R' engine.

upper-deck dining room could accommodate 50 passengers at a sitting, double-berthed sleeping cabins were available, there were cubicles with wash basins and hot and cold water, and even a small lower-deck smoking room. This was sheer luxury by comparison with contemporary airliners, and the R.34 of ten years earlier had shown that even safe transatlantic travel was within the craft's capability.

The beginning of a great era of travel seemed to have dawned: one passenger to fly in the R.101 was quoted in the *The Times* of 17 December 1929: '...the airship is steadier than the train; quieter than the aeroplane; less given to rolling than the sea-going ships. She has all of the virtues of these three and others of her own... Her movements are deliberate, her progress serene.' Less than twelve months later, on 5 October 1930, the R.101 was but smouldering wreckage in a field near Beauvais, France. Of the 54 people on board for this first Britain-India flight, 48 were killed or died of their injuries. With them died all British interest in the airship as a commercial vehicle.

Germany had, of course, far greater experience in the construction of rigid airships. Her *Graf Zeppelin*, launched in 1928, was a superb craft and one which had a highly successful 12-year history before being scrapped. The first of many

significant achievements was a return flight from Friedrichsahfen to Lakehurst, New Jersey, at the end of October 1928. During 1929 she completed a round-the-world trip of 21,500 miles (34,600 km) in 21 days, this including a non-stop 7,000-mile (11,265 km) stage from Friedrichshafen to Tokyo. Then, in 1932, she began to fly regularly across the South Atlantic from Friedrichshafen to Recife, and eventually to Rio de Janeiro. When her service days were over the *Graf Zeppelin*, undoubtedly the world's most successful passenger airship, had carried some 13,100 passengers and flown well over a million miles.

We must consider the reason for this emphasis on ocean crossings. Thinking men had long believed that improved means of international communication would speed civilization, universal understanding and worldwide peace. The aeroplane seemed to offer the means for realizing these hopes, but only if intercontinental travel became feasible and commonplace. Jacques Schneider must have had similar thoughts in mind when, in 1912, he had first offered his trophy for international competition between water borne aircraft.

Seven-tenths of the earth's surface is covered by water and it was reasonable to assume that development of effi-

Below: A picture that
might well have been
entitled 'Ancient and
Modern'; a Cierva 'Auto-
giro' is caught in midair
with a backcloth of
Hampton Court Palace.

Above left: A painting by
Kenneth McDonough of
an Imperial Airways
Handley Page W.8b being
taxied across Plough Lane,
Croydon.

Left: Original biplane
designs were beginning to
emerge from the American
industry, such as this
Waco 9 which had a
welded steel-tube fuselage
structure. But it was
gravely underpowered and
was described as 'a failure
looking for somewhere to
happen'.

Above: In America, utilizing the corrugated skin
type of construction
pioneered by Junkers in
Germany, the Ford com-
pany produced what
became an enduring air-
craft known officially as
the Ford Tri-motor. Still
flying today, it soon ac-
quired the better-known
name of 'Tin Goose'.

Left: Most successful of the world's passenger-carrying rigid airships was the German *Graf Zeppelin*, which had flown well over a million miles before being retired. It is shown here as it landed at Hanworth Park, Middlesex.

Right: Few flying-boats can create a more impressive picture than the Dornier Do X seen on take-off. It was powered by 12 600 hp Curtiss Conqueror engines.

Below right: Short S.8 Calcutta G-EBVH *City of Athens*, later renamed *City of Stonehaven*, one of the fleet that Imperial Airways used for a weekly Britain-India service in 1929.

cient aircraft, which could operate from, and land on, water surfaces, would do much to speed the development of intercontinental travel. Even a forced landing would be less of a hazard if the machine could alight on the sea and ride the waves until help arrived. There were also many who believed that the yielding surface of the water would offer greater chances of survival in a crash, by comparison with the rigid face of Mother Earth.

The Schneider Trophy Races, which had started quietly enough in 1913 and 1914, were interrupted by World War I and still retained something of the atmosphere of a local sports meeting when resumed in 1919. Only in their latter years did they become a symbol of international prestige, attracting worldwide attention. Britain finally won and retained the Trophy in 1931 with the Supermarine S.6B monoplane seaplane which recorded a speed of over 340 mph (547 km/h).

This emancipation of the once frail seaplane made commercial operators think on similar lines, leading to the development of large passenger-carrying flying-boats. Imperial Airways began with Short Calcuttas, which could carry fifteen passengers, and on 30 March 1929 started a weekly Britain-India service that offered seven days of varied travel for those with £130 to spare for the single fare. First leg of the route was by Armstrong Whitworth Argosy from Croydon to Basle. Basle was linked to Genoa by a train journey, and at Genoa the Calcuttas filled in the next leg to Alexandria. From there, D.H.66 Hercules landplanes completed the journey to Karachi.

It was more than a flight, it was adventure with a capital A; especially when night stops were made at such exciting places as Foreign Legion-type forts in areas where the Arabs were far from sociable. Those lucky enough to afford such trips certainly had value for their money: memories to last a lifetime and a fund of after-dinner stories that would keep their friends well entertained for months.

Germany, too, was interested in the potential of large flying-boats, especially to link the Old and New Worlds separated by the North Atlantic. For her it was primarily a question of prestige, and she launched what was then the biggest aeroplane ever built: the Dornier Do X. With a wing span of 157 ft 5 in (48.00 m), maximum take-off weight of 123,460 lb (56,000 kg) and accommodation for a crew of ten and up to 170 passengers, it needed the power of ten 525 hp Siemens Jupiter air-cooled engines to get it into the air. These proved inadequate, suffering loss of power from over-heating. Even when replaced by twelve 600 hp Curtiss Conqueror water-cooled engines power was still marginal, and a ten-month technically-plagued trip to North and South America ended of its development.

The solution to regular and reliable transoceanic crossings was still in the future. The provision of fast, scheduled services within Europe and Australia was still unresolved. This latter country, with centres of civilization separated by long distances of difficult terrain, was keenly interrested in the scope of air travel.

With a single Avro 504K (G-AUBG), the Queensland and Northern Territory Aerial Services Ltd., now known universally as Qantas, and first registered on 16 November 1920, began to operate charter and pleasure trips. Its roots were planted deep and its branches spread rapidly: by 1926 it had become the first airline in the world to build and operate its own aircraft. Two years later, on 15 May 1928, it inaugurated the world's first Flying Doctor Service. By 1933 Qantas aircraft had already flown more than two million miles.

Above: The Douglas DC-3
Dakota, which first flew in
1935 and still serves with
many airlines in 1973, has
become welcome the
world over: even in the
frozen wastes of Lapland.

Right: The Boeing Model
247, one of aviation's
historic aeroplanes, gave
birth in 1933 to the mod-
ern transport aircraft.

But it was in America that the most vital seed of civil aviation had germinated, right at the close of the decade. On 8 February 1933 a strange-looking monoplane made its maiden flight at Seattle, Washington: strange-looking because it was so unlike the high-wing three-engined Fords that had become commonplace, standing high on their ungainly fixed-wing landing gear.

By comparison this new aeroplane, known as the Boeing Model 247, was a good-looking low-wing monoplane of all-metal construction, with two cleanly-cowled engines and landing gear which could be retracted in flight. The improved Model 247D, with 550 hp Pratt & Whitney radial engines, variable-pitch propellers and other refinements, began to revolutionize transcontinental travel in America. United Air Lines' (UAL) 247Bs chopped $6\frac{3}{4}$ hours off the coast-to-coast schedule of their chief rival, Transcontinental and Western Air (TWA). With passengers preferring to travel the faster UAL route, it was not unexpected that TWA would also want to order the Boeing machines.

Unfortunately for TWA, there was a financial link between Boeing and UAL. When the answer was 'no sale', TWA had to find an alternative, but quickly. Their specification requirements, presented to the Douglas Aircraft Company, resulted in the first flight of a competing prototype, on 1 July 1933. Designated as the DC-1, it was superior to the Model 247 in several ways: when a developed version entered service at the beginning of the next decade it was to revolutionize air travel.

The years 1924–33 had indeed been a decade of progress, much of it stemming from a far more scientific approach to the problems of flight. It was also a decade which had witnessed the beginnings of new ideas that would have great importance in the future. Juan de la Cierva's *Autogiro* has already been mentioned; others deserve recording even though they then represented embryonic ideas.

For example, at the Royal Aircraft Establishment (RAE), Farnborough, Dr. A.A. Griffith had begun experimentation to discover the potential of a gas turbine for aircraft propulsion (1926–8). On 24 September 1929 Lt. James Doolittle of the US Army Air Corps had flown a Consolidated NY-2 biplane 'blind', using a new sensitive altimeter, gyro-stabilized artificial horizon and direction indicator, developed by Lawrence Sperry. On 30 September 1929 the German, Fritz von Opel, had flown a rocket-powered glider at speeds of up to 100 mph (161 km/h). Also in Germany, on 14 May 1931, a group of students belonging to the *Verein fur Raumschiffahrt* (VfR, Society for Space Travel), launched their first successful liquid-propellant rocket. A leading figure of the group was named Wernher von Braun.

The next decade promised a great deal of interest.

Never-to-be-forgotten in
British aviation history
is the Supermarine Spit-
fire, designed by R.J.
Mitchell.

Inset: The Spitfire and
Hawker Hurricane were
to give British victory in
what became known as
the Battle of Britain. The
very essence of the conflict
is retained for posterity in
this atmospheric painting
by Paul Nash.

Above: Second place in
the MacRoberston Eng-
land-Australia Air Race
went, surprisingly, to a
DC-2 of KLM. Willing
hands help haul it out of a
sticky landing field en
route to Melbourne.

Right: Superb flying-boats
like the Short S.23 'Empire
Boat' were soon to make
air communications be-
tween England and Aus-
tralia almost routine.
Canopus being refuelled at
Dar-es-Salaam.

WINGS
OVER
THE OCEANS
1934·43

how little do you think
On the dangers of the seas
Martin Parker

The surface of the sea appears to be covered with great white motion-less palm-trees, palms marked with ribs and seams stiff in a sort of frost . . . like a splintered mirror. The hours during which a man flies over this mirror are hours in which there is no assurance of the possession of anything in the world. These palms beneath the plane are so many poisoned flowers. (Antoine de Saint Exupéy)

Minutes passed, then hours, and still there was nothing but sea all round. Looking over the side of the cockpit I could see the shapes of sharks, so for my peace of mind kept my eyes glued on the compass, set for Bathurst Island. After an infinity of time I saw land ahead. I refused to believe it and would not look for ten minutes . . . This sea was quite the most awful experience of my life . . . I hate and loathe the Timor Sea. (C.W.A. Scott)

The real task was to find the island, and before sunset too . . . looking ahead, I found pieces of the horizon cut out by dark grey rain clouds; they squatted on the sea surface like shapeless fungus on the top of a log. Bad weather! My God! that was too much. I suddenly felt emptied of all courage; I touched the utter depths of cowardliness. I was so terribly helpless, totally unable to lift a finger to keep off the death I could see inexorably closing in on me. (Francis Chichester)

The Southern Cross *was encrusted with ice; our radio had failed; and we were alone in the midst of the deserted Tasman Sea. It was pitch black; we could see nothing, hear nothing. We did not know where we were. I think that night I touched the extreme of human fear. Panic was very near, and I almost lost my head. I felt a desire to pull her round, dive – climb – do anything, to escape – We were like rats in a trap . . . (Sir Charles Kingsford-Smith)*

These are the words of four brave men, pioneers of the air-lanes which we, today, can travel quickly, safely and comfortably. They suffered to grasp hold of the dreams ever beckoning them on into the blue sky. We owe them much for their endurance and fortitude.

The seas were the great challenge. For years men had been navigating their surface in vessels of all kinds. Perhaps it seemed logical that a boat with wings was the prime need of the new air age. In the event, this became the decade of the flying-boat. But before this came about American aircraft were beginning to take a lead in civil aviation.

The DC-1 prototype which had flown in 1933 was so promising that an improved version, designated DC-2, was put into production by the Douglas Company. This was

able to carry 14 passengers and also introduced trailing-edge flaps, which gave improved take-off and landing performance. And when American Airlines, an early customer for the DC-2, wanted a sleeper version, Douglas introduced the DST (Douglas Sleeper Transport) which had a wider fuselage. The day version of the same model, which could accommodate an extra fore and aft row of seats to make it a 21-seater, was known as the DC-3.

This aircraft completely revolutionized air travel in America. It was powered originally by two 1000 hp Wright Cyclone engines, but these were soon changed for 1,200 hp Pratt & Whitney Twin Wasps, giving it the capability of maintaining altitude with a full load on the power of one engine. So outstanding was this aircraft that by the time America entered World War II in December 1941, no less than 80 per cent of all scheduled airline services in America were being flown by DC-3s. More remarkable, perhaps, was the fact that in a twelve-month period during 1939–40 the user airlines recorded a 100 per cent safety record.

At this same period in Europe, the British, Dutch, French and Italian nations, all of whom had colonial possessions, were busy stretching their wings towards the east. Britain's Imperial Airways, linking at Singapore with Australia's Qantas, forged the final link of a 12,722 mile (20,474 km) route that provided an air bridge between these two Commonwealth countries. In 1934 the Christmas mail was flown over this route for the first time, taking almost two weeks.

There was still much scope for improvement, and an Australian patriot, Sir William Macpherson Robertson, sought to encourage the development of faster air links with the mother country. The bait was a £15,000 prize for an air race but, surprisingly, it aroused little interest initially. So far as aircraft manufacturers were concerned, it meant they would have to build a special machine of good speed and range if they were to have a reasonable chance of winning. And that would cost far more than the prize money.

There was, of course, the prestige that would attach to the builder of the winning aeroplane, and this swayed the issue. One of the interested companies was de Havilland, who designed and built three examples of a twin-engined aircraft which they designated the D.H.88 Comet. The first ma-

Right: One of the most vital aircraft in America's armoury at the beginning of her involvement in World War II was the Boeing B-17 Flying Fortress.

Inset: Wartime aircraft had many different shapes and sizes. The Westland Lysander, intended primarily for army co-operation, provided memorable cloak-and-dagger operations setting down and picking up agents in German-occupied France.

chine made its maiden flight only six weeks before the start of the race. There was little time for testing and modification, but with a potential speed of over 230 mph (370 km/h) and a range of 2,900 miles (4,667 km) it clearly had a good chance of winning.

The gamble paid off. Flown by C.W.A. Scott and T. Campbell Black, the Comet G-ACSS was first home in the speed race. But the second aircraft home, and winner of the handicap race, was a Douglas DC-2 which had been entered by the Dutch national airline, KLM. Flown by K.D. Parmentier and J.J. Moll, it also carried three passengers and 421 lb (191 kg) of air mail, and completed the journey in 3 days 18 hr 17 min. To use the phrase of an old-fashioned parlour game: the consequence was that de Havilland got some prestige, Imperial Airways got a shock, and the Douglas Aircraft Company received an order for fourteen more DC-2s from KLM. It marked the first major entry of American civil aircraft into the European scene, giving a lead which the United States has retained ever since.

Britain could not take this lying down. While the Dutch were awaiting their DC-2s, the British government an-

nounced on 20 December 1934 the introduction of an Empire Air Mail Scheme. This meant that henceforth all mail to or from Commonwealth countries would be carried by air. To enable Imperial Airways to cope with the programme a fleet of four-engined flying-boats were ordered from Short Brothers.

Thus emerged the Short S.23, designated the 'C-class' by Imperial Airways, but known universally as the Empire Boat. It was a superb flying-boat, with accommodation for a crew of three or four, up to 24 passengers and stowage for $1\frac{1}{2}$ tons of mail. Powered by four 910 hp Bristol Pegasus engines it had a maximum speed of 200 mph (322 km/h) at 5,500 ft (1,680 m), which was pretty fair for a flying-boat of the 1930s which grossed over 18 tons at take-off.

The first of the breed, *Canopus*, flew for the first time on 3 July 1936, and made its first scheduled service flight on 30 October. By the end of 1937 Imperial Airways had received 22 Empire Boats, and by the end of June 1938 it was possible to fly from their flying-boat base at Hythe, on Southampton Water, to Sydney, Australia, without changing aircraft.

Left and right: A British idea to conquer the North Atlantic route was the *Maia–Mercury* composite, shown here immediately after separation.

Below: Even if it was possible to travel by air from England to Australia, the much shorter distance between England and America was a far more formidable barrier. German attempts to bridge the North Atlantic included mid-ocean depot ships which could retrieve, refuel and launch big seaplanes like this Blohm & Voss Ha 139 on the *Schwabenland's* catapult.

In America similar lines of thought had prompted Pan American Airways to order flying-boats to span the vast reaches of the Pacific. She hedged her bets, ordering from two manufacturers simultaneously, and thus acquired Martin M.130s and Sikorsky S.42s. To the Martin boat, *China Clipper*, fell the honour of making the inaugural mail flight across the central Pacific. Her initial trip from San Francisco to Manila, Philippines, via Honolulu, Midway, Wake and Guam, took six days; but it was not until 21 October 1936 that scheduled passenger services were initiated.

World travel by air was on the up and up. The fly in the ointment was the North Atlantic, which was plagued by bad weather that posed severe navigational problems, and also had a west-east airstream that did nothing to help east-west crossing. This explains why in the early 1930s France, Germany and Italy concentrated on the conquest of the South Atlantic, using the Dakar-Brazil route which in the main enjoyed good weather conditions. By 1936 the French Aeropostale, later merged into Air France, offered a regular service from Toulouse to Santiago. Germany's Lufthansa adopted a compromise of aircraft, ship and aircraft for her Stuttgart-Rio de Janeiro route.

But at this period the *Graf Zeppelin* was flying regularly across the South Atlantic. The larger *Hindenburg*, 814 ft (248 m), appeared to offer the capability of a regular prestigious North Atlantic service. Those hopes ended disastrously when the *Hindenburg*, after several successful transatlantic flights, was consumed in all-enveloping flame as she came to her mooring mast at Lakehurst, New Jersey, on 6 May 1937. It was the end of German commercial airship services, the *Graf Zeppelin* being put into retirement.

Germany was to continue with determined efforts to conquer the North Atlantic, her transatlantic liners *Bremen* and *Europa* being equipped with catapults to launch a mail-carrying Heinkel seaplane when the vessels were some 300 miles (483 km) from their destination. This provided a $4\frac{1}{2}$-day sea/air mail service between Germany and New York but was, at best, an unsatifactory compromise for those who wanted to see passengers and air mail being carried safely over what has been called 'the cruel sea'.

The Germans next tackled the problem by stationing a depot ship off the Azores, which could retrieve, refuel and catapult off a Blohm & Voss Ha 139 seaplane, and in 1937 14 scheduled flights were operated successfully. It was still a compromise. During 1938 another 26 scheduled flights were made using the same technique, but it was not until 11 August 1938 that a Focke-Wulf Fw 200 Condor made an Atlantic crossing via Hamburg, Glasgow and Newfoundland to New York. Other experimental flights with the Condor were to follow, but the approach of World War II

Below: Almost on the eve of World War II, America was to gain leadership over the North Atlantic using Boeing Model 314 *Clippers*.

ended DLH's hopes of inaugurating a scheduled North Atlantic passenger service.

Britain and America, both possessing long-range flying-boats, decided to initiate simultaneous survey flights. On 5 July 1937 Pan American's *Clipper III* took off from Botwood, Newfoundland, bound for Foynes on Ireland's River Shannon, while Imperial Airways' Empire Boat *Caledonia* climbed away from the Shannon. Both made uneventful crossings, followed by successful return flights to their own countries.

British attempts to complete a North Atlantic bridge included such ideas as the 'pick-a-back' concept of Robert Mayo. This involved a short S.23, the *Maia*, modified to carry on its back a specially designed seaplane, *Mercury*. The thinking behind such an apparently odd scheme was based on the knowledge that an aircraft would remain airborne safely at a weight considerably higher than that at which it could take off. Consequently, if you could air-launch a well-laden aircraft, this extra load in the form of fuel would offer increased range.

Following such a take-off from Foynes, on 20 July 1938, *Mercury* made a record crossing to Montreal in the capable hands of Capt. D.C.T. Bennett. But like the German experiments, prior to the Condor flights, this was no more than a compromise. Range was still the problem, and during 1939 experiments were made with flight refuelling techniques. Two Handley Page Harrows, converted as tankers, suckled the Empire Boats *Cabot* and *Caribou*, enabling these aircraft to make eight successful return trips over the Atlantic. But no passengers were carried and the honour of inaugurating

the first regular scheduled transatlantic passenger service went to America.

Boeing's 42-ton Model 314 flying-boats ordered by Pan American Airways provided the answer to the problem. With a still air range in excess of 3,000 miles (4,828 km), they first went into passenger service over the Atlantic on 8 July 1939.

By that date the long-threatening clouds of another European war were beginning to darken the horizon. How well had the aircraft industry, which had conquered the world's oceans in the space of 36 years, prepared itself for a new and, predictably, horrifying war in the air?

At the beginning of this decade Adolf Hitler had arrived on the political scene in Germany, determined to create a new all-powerful German empire. Forbidden by the Versailles Treaty to have military aircraft, the Germans gradually built up a clandestine air force. Medium-range bombers such as the Dornier Do 17, Heinkel He III and Junkers Ju 88 first saw service as civil transports for Lufthansa. The Junkers Ju 87 Stuka (dive bomber) and Messerschmitt Bf 109 fighter were evolved behind a veil of secrecy.

Britain's participation in the Schneider Trophy Races had led to the superb S.6B, progenitor of R.J. Mitchell's Supermarine Spitfire. Sydney Camm's no less famous Hawker Hurricane had derived from the Air Ministry's 1934 specification for a four-gun monoplane fighter to replace the biplane Hawker Fury. Nor had the provision of a bomber force been neglected. The Bristol Blenheim, Handley Page Hampden and Vickers Wellington repre-

Left: Germany had long
been preparing for war,
and aircraft like the Junkers Ju 88 began to enter
service in civil guise. It became operational in many
roles and the Ju 88P-2
version, with two 37 mm
cannon in a ventral turret,
is illustrated.

Above: Most famous of
the German wartime bom-
bers was the Do 17 'flying
pencil', evolved originally
as a six-passenger high-
speed mail 'plane for Lufthansa. A slightly larger
version, the Dornier Do
217, also saw extensive service and a 217E is seen
before a night take-off.

sented the latest monoplane medium-range bombers. Already on the drawing boards were embryo four-engined long-range strategic bombers that would emerge eventually as the never-to-be-forgotten Halifax, Lancaster and Stirling.

In the between-war years France had fallen behind in the development of advanced aircraft, and isolationist America had been concerned with civil rather than military types. Typical of United States Army fighters of the period were the Boeing P-26, Curtiss P-36 and Seversky P-35; unfortunately they compared unfavourably with contemporary British and German fighters. But stemming from civil aircraft development was one important monoplane bomber, the Boeing B-17 Flying Fortress. Despite the craft's potential, the United States Navy's stubborn insistence that only the Navy should be responsible for the defence of America's shores was to result in far too few of these valuable aircraft being available when America entered the war.

Japan, involved in war with China, had been steadily improving her aircraft. Lack of technical knowledge had forced her to rely initially upon copying the products of Western nations. The demands of war and imposed sanctions forced her to begin to evolve original designs. Because of her island homeland these stressed the development of carrier-based aircraft. This led ultimately to some excellent machines, in particular the Mitsubishi A6M Zero fighter, which took part in almost every major action of the war in the Pacific theatre.

The Italian invasion of Abyssinia (Ethiopia) in 1935, and German and Italian participation in the Spanish Civil War (1938) had left few illusions as to the scenes of death and destruction that war from the air would bring. The worst fears were soon confirmed when the German Luftwaffe and Wehrmacht stormed across Europe, and England stood alone against her armed might. The turning point was the Battle of Britain; the loss of Germany's most experienced pilots having a profound effect on the ultimate course of the war in Europe.

Right: Maid-of-all-work of the British bomber squadrons in the early days was the Vickers Wellington, known affectionately as the 'Wimpy'. Its unique geodetic fuselage structure, designed by Barnes Wallis, enabled it to survive strong enemy attacks.

Above: Prime defensive weapons of the British RAF at the beginning of the war were the Spitfire and Hurricane. A squadron of Hawker Hurricane II Bs climbs over the patchwork quilt of the English countryside.

Right: Britain's four-engined heavy bombers, the Halifax, Lancaster and Stirling, were to pound Germany round-the-clock in partnership with the USAAF's B.17s and B-24 Liberators. Against a background of the setting sun, a squadron of Lancasters prepares for the night's work.

At the height of the Battle, when asked by Reichsmar-
schall Göring what was his most urgent requirement, Adolf
Galland had replied: 'I should like an outfit of Spitfires for
my group.' Later, when Hitler's 'Fortress Europe' was
being blasted day and night by American and British four-
engined bombers, President Roosevelt was to comment
that: 'Hitler forgot to put a roof over his fortress.' In fact,
the roof had not been forgotten: the RAF's Churchillian
'Few' had already weakened its supporting timbers.

This was a war of technical innovation speeded by a
need to counter the scientific advances of both sides. Radio
communication and navigation aids attained new heights
of efficiency and accuracy; radar made it possible to see the
hitherto invisible; new techniques and weapons were being
developed that would change forever the traditional
concepts of warfare.

On 30 June 1939 the German Heinkel He 176 became
the world's first aircraft to fly with a liquid-propellant
rocket motor and two months later, on 27 August, the
Heinkel He 178 became the world's first aircraft to fly with
a turbojet engine. It was not until 15 May 1941 that the
British Gloster E. 28/39, powered by Frank Whittle's turbojet engine, flew for the first time.

When Japanese carrier-based aircraft struck at Pearl
Harbour on 7 December 1941, virtually eliminating the
United States Pacific Fleet, what had until then been a
European war exploded into a worldwide conflict. British
and American air defences in the Pacific theatre were
pathetically weak, both nations still trying to maintain an
outmoded belief that naval power was supreme. When the
British battleships HMS *Prince of Wales* and HMS *Repulse*
were also sunk by enemy air action three days later, the
whole balance of power in the Pacific passed into Japanese
hands.

It was clear that air rather than naval power had become
supreme. As combatant nations sought to gain ascendancy
new and more terrifying weapons were to be developed. If
Horace Walpole could have risen from the grave he might
have been forgiven for saying: 'I told you so.' Back in 1783,
when the Montgolfier brothers had first 'conquered' the
air, he had written to a friend:

'I hope these new mechanic meteors will prove only
playthings for the learned and the idle, and not be converted into new engines of destruction for the human race.'

Left: It seems hardly possible that in the first of the
three years 1939–41 the
German Heinkel He 178
made the first flight of a
turbojet-powered aircraft,
and that in the last the
Gloster-Whittle E.28/39,
illustrated, flew for the first
time at RAF Cranwell.

Right: The Gloster-Whittle
E. 28/39 led to Britain's
first operational jet aircraft, the Gloster Meteor.
Similarly, in Germany the
Messerschmitt Me 262,
shown here, was develop-
ed – the first jet aircraft to
enter operational service
with the Luftwaffe.

THROUGH THE BARRIER 1944:53

Left: Against the German V1, Gloster Meteors, the first operational turbojet fighters in the world, scored considerable success. Illustrated are Meteor NF.14s of the RAF, the last production version with extended nose radome.

Right: The German V2 rocket, shown here on a mobile launcher, was a far more potent weapon, against which there was no defence once it had been launched.

the age of speed grows, men have taken wings and no bounds can be set to their audacity . . .
Michael Burn

. . . A smoke cartridge hissed into the sky. Its green track over Test Stand VII drifted sluggishly away before the wind. Ten seconds more. The picture on the television screen was unchanged.

'Ignition!'

The propulsion engineer must have pulled the first of the three main levers. I noticed on the television picture that clouds were issuing from the nozzle mouth. Sparks rained through them, bounced off the blast deflector and scattered over the concrete platform on which the firing table stood.

'Preliminary!'

The rain of sparks rapidly coalesced to a flame and changed in a second into a leaping stream of reddish-yellow gas. The flame of the eight-ton stage of thrust developed. The power of this preliminary stage was not yet sufficient to lift the 13.5 ton rocket from the firing table . . .

'Cleared!'

The propulsion engineer had pulled the third and last main lever. Release of the casting-off cable ushered in the principal stage. A turbo-pump of 4,000 revolutions a minute and a capacity of 540 horse-power came into play, forcing 33 gallons of oxygen and alcohol per second into the combustion chamber of the rocket motor.

After about a second, thrust rose to 25 tons. With an acceleration practically corresponding to that of a falling stone, the rocket climbed straight and steadily upwards from the firing table and disappeared from the television screen, leaving behind it an immense whirling cloud of dust.

This is how Maj. Gen. Walter Dornberger described the first successful launch of the German A4 rocket, on 3 October 1942, better known to the Allies as the V2, (V for *Vergeltungswaffe*, reprisal weapon, No.2.). It was not until the evening of 8 September 1944 that mysterious explosions shook the London suburbs of Chiswick and Epping almost simultaneously as the first of these long-range missiles reached their target. Mysterious they were indeed, for travelling at some 3,500 mph (5,630 km/h) at impact, they arrived way ahead of the sound of their approach.

There was no defence against the V2 once it had been launched. Not only was its speed too great, but its trajectory carried it out of Earth's atmosphere. The only possible defence was attack against its launching sites.

It had been preceded by the V1, a very different weapon:

a true flying-bomb, a conventional-looking small mid-wing monoplane powered by an unusual pulse-jet engine. Its power plant provided the characteristic noise which soon had the British giving it the nickname 'buzz-bomb', or sometimes 'doodlebug'. However, the V1 travelled at only some 350 mph (563 km/h) at altitudes between 600 and 6,000 feet (183–1830 m), making it vulnerable to more advanced fighter aircraft and ground-based anti-aircraft defences. Fortunately for the Allies, both these weapons entered service too late to change the outcome of the war in Europe.

Advanced versions of the Spitfire and the new Hawker Typhoon scored their successes against the V1, and on 27 July 1944 Gloster Meteor jet-powered fighters joined these operations for the first time; thus the Meteors made history as being the world's first operational jet fighters. The German Messerschmitt Me 262A-1a did not make its true operational debut until 3 October 1944, in attacks on USAAF bomber formations.

In the closing stages of the war in the European theatre, Allied air superiority was the dominating factor. The combined effects of strategic bombing and the rapid westward advance of the Russian forces gave rise to a situation where,

75

Below: In the latter phase of World War II Igor Sikorsky achieved his ambition to create a practical single-rotor helicopter. This YR-4 prototype developed rapidly into a valuable addition to the aviation scene.

Below: In the closing stages of the Pacific War, USAAF Boeing B-29 Superfortresses began the systematic destruction of Japan's industrial cities. This picture of Hamamatsu shows how vulnerable they were to incendiary attacks.

despite the availability of immense numbers of operational aircraft, the Luftwaffe became impotent as its life-giving supplies of aviation fuel dwindled to a trickle. The inevitable conclusion came on 7 May 1945, when terms of unconditional surrender were signed at Rheims, the following day becoming known as V.E. Day (Victory Europe).

But war in the Pacific theatre was then reaching its crescendo as the huge Boeing B-29 Superfortresses burnt out the hearts of major cities on the Japanese homeland. The initial deployment of these bombers had met with comparatively little success. Unpredictable weather, high speed winds at the operational altitude of the Superforts, spirited Japanese fighter defence, and disappointing bombing accuracy had shown little achievement for considerable cost. Only when new techniques were introduced by Maj.-Gen. Curtis E. LeMay did the B-29 realize its potential.

LeMay's solution was low-level night attack, using a Pathfinder group for initial target illumination. That this plan was correct was proved on the night of 9/10 March 1945 when 334 B-29s set out to bomb Tokyo. Post-raid analysis showed that 15.8 square miles (40.92 km²) had been burnt out of the heart of the city. The official death roll was 83,793, with another 40,918 injured and 1,008,005 rendered homeless. This was the world's most devastating air attack of all time, not even exceeded by the atom bomb attacks on Hiroshima and Nagasaki on 6 August and 9 August 1945, which brought the end of World War II a few days later.

Whereas World War I had resulted in improvement in

77

Below: Air cargo formed
an important part of the
post-war civil aviation
build-up, although many
people thought Silver
City's cross-Channel air
ferry for motor cars a little
ambitious.

Right: The first clash of
the 'cold war' between
East and West manifested
itself in the Berlin Airlift.
C-47s line up for unload-
ing at Tempelhof Airport
in what became known as
'Operation Vittles'.

the capability of the aeroplane, this last global conflict demonstrated that an aircraft carrying the newly-developed atom bomb was a supreme weapon. It has been argued that those dropped on Japan were superfluous to the outcome of the war, that the nation had already been brought to its knees by 'conventional' weapons. Nonetheless, operational deployment of this horrifying weapon brought a realization of its power that no number of controlled tests could have achieved. The sacrifices of Hiroshima and Nagasaki may prove sufficient to ensure that mankind will never have to face a third world war.

Technological advances had been enormous: new methods of construction made possible robust and reliable airframes; piston-engines reached the zenith of their development and the first turbine engines were beginning to give some hint of their potential; radio and redar progressed to a point where the prospect of accurate, all-weather navigation was just around the corner. Yet another type of aircraft had become practical when Igor Sikorsky flew his prototype VS-300 single-rotor helicopter, leading to the Sikorsky R-4, which made its appearance in the closing stages of the war.

More significant was the development in America of the reliable long-range transport aircraft needed to sustain and support her forces stretched out across the length and breadth of the Pacific Ocean. All around the world airfields with long, paved runways had proliferated for the operation of these new, large aircraft. They spelled the end of the flying-boats which had carried passengers and air mail over the intercontinental airlanes before the war.

This was inevitable, for an airline operating flying-boat services had some hefty and now-avoidable overheads to meet. There was the costly business of maintaining ocean terminals: ensuring the seaway was clear of floating debris, provision of 'boat to shore' transport, passenger lounges, refreshment and other facilities. By comparison, the landing fee charged at a municipally-owned airport was a petty cash item.

No crystal ball was needed to foresee an enormous expansion in air travel. During the war hundreds of thousands of men and women had come to accept transport by air as routine. If the post-war airlines could carry them on business or for pleasure at realistic fares, it would not be long before the airlancs would carry the bulk of transcontinental and intercontinental passengers.

The pattern of wartime aviation had developed in such a way that America was in the best position to take advantage of this new market. The European nations had necessarily had to concentrate on the design of short-range or medium-range combat aircraft. The United States, on the other hand, concerned with the transport and succour of troops thousands of miles from the homeland, had developed large, long-range aircraft that were easily convertible to carry civilian passengers during the interim period before new civil transports emerged. Additionally, they had taken a fairly firm hold on this particular market before the war began.

Thus the B-29 Superfortress which had carried havoc to the Japanese, sired the Boeing Model 377 Stratocruiser.

Right: Faster and faster, was the cry. Advanced research was needed to penetrate the 'sound barrier': the little Bell X-1 research aircraft in which 'Chuck' Yeager achieved the first supersonic flight beneath the belly of its Boeing B-29 'mother plane'.

Far right: Air cargo soon became big business. Operators would carry anything, anywhere: but some loads presented unusual problems.

When Pan American first introduced this aircraft on the North Atlantic route it set completely new standards of luxury and comfort for its passengers.

The moment had arrived for a new era of peaceful aviation; the dream which had spurred on the pioneers from their first brief 'hops'. Yet almost before the scene had been set, was shattered. On 26 June 1948 the Russian closed the land routes to West Berlin, hoping to force the British, French and American allies to withdraw their occupying forces from the city, which had become virtually an island surrounded by the Russian Zone at the end of World War II. But although the Soviets stopped access by road and rail, the Allies were determined to maintain the $2\frac{1}{4}$ million occupants of West Berlin by air. The almost constant roar of aircraft, which three years earlier had brought terror to the hearts of the Berliners, was now the triumphant note of salvation. If the Russians had expected it to dwindle after a first token attempt at relief, they were to be disappointed.

Food and medical supplies were priority cargoes but with the onset of winter, coal, fuel oil and petrol began to assume an increasing tonnage. Nothing could deter the efforts of the Allies and the individual aircrews dedicated to this task, not even one of the worst winters that Europe had suffered for several years. USAF transport aircraft alone carried in 234,500 tons of supplies during April 1949, and in the face of such determination it is not surprising that on 12 May the Russians realized that their gambit was unsuccessful, and re-opened the surface routes.

The cost had been enormous, including the tragic and unneccessary loss of 51 aircrew. The gain had been even greater, demonstrating positively to the Eastern bloc that the Western powers considered no cost too great to maintain a state of peace.

Power politics apart, the Berlin Airlift had emphasized, if emphasis was needed, the capabilities of modern transport aircraft. Businessmen around the world were given a practical demonstration of the cargo-carrying capacity now available to them. In the past, aircraft had been used to speed urgent commodities like medical supplies, perishable goods, spare parts, newspapers and, of course, air mail. They had also been used for cargoes like precious metals and gems, their high altitude transit making it unlikely they could be snatched by the most cunning thief.

Now all this was changed. There was little doubt that aeroplanes would be able to carry anything that could be manoeuvred into their cargo holds; and it did not take long for the aviation industry to devise special aircraft able to contain almost unbelievable loads. It was therefore no surprise when, in 1948, Britain's Silver City Airways inaugurated a car ferry across the English Channel. Soon thousands of travellers discovered that the saving in time slightly increased cost compared to sea travel made the slightly increased cost well worthwhile.

It has long been appreciated by those who operate air services that passengers will almost invariably choose to travel by the aircraft that offers the quickest transit time over a given route. There is, after all, little of interest to be seen from the operating altitude of modern airliners, and the faster travel time gives increased scope for business or enjoyment at the end of the journey.

During this fifth decade of powered flight the quest had become speed. Man could already build reliable aircraft capable of circumnavigating the globe which was his habitat. It was logical to assume that the greatest financial rewards were reserved for those who could provide the fastest travel.

There were snags. The potential of piston engines and propeller propulsion was at its peak. The turbojet engine was in its infancy. Advanced propeller-driven fighter aircraft had encountered severe aerodynamic buffeting when approaching terminal velocity in a dive. It was so violent that many pilots lost their lives when wings or tail units parted company with the basic aircraft structure.

If the full potential of the new turbine power plants was to be realized, it was necessary to penetrate this aerodynamic 'barrier' to flight at higher speeds. Aerodynamicists soon discovered that when the airflow over the wing of an aircraft approached the speed of sound (760 mph: 1223 km/h at sea level, falling to 660 mph: 1,062 km/h above 36,000 ft: 10,975 m) its smooth flow became broken up into shock waves that were responsible for the violent buffeting.

German wartime research had shown that swept wings

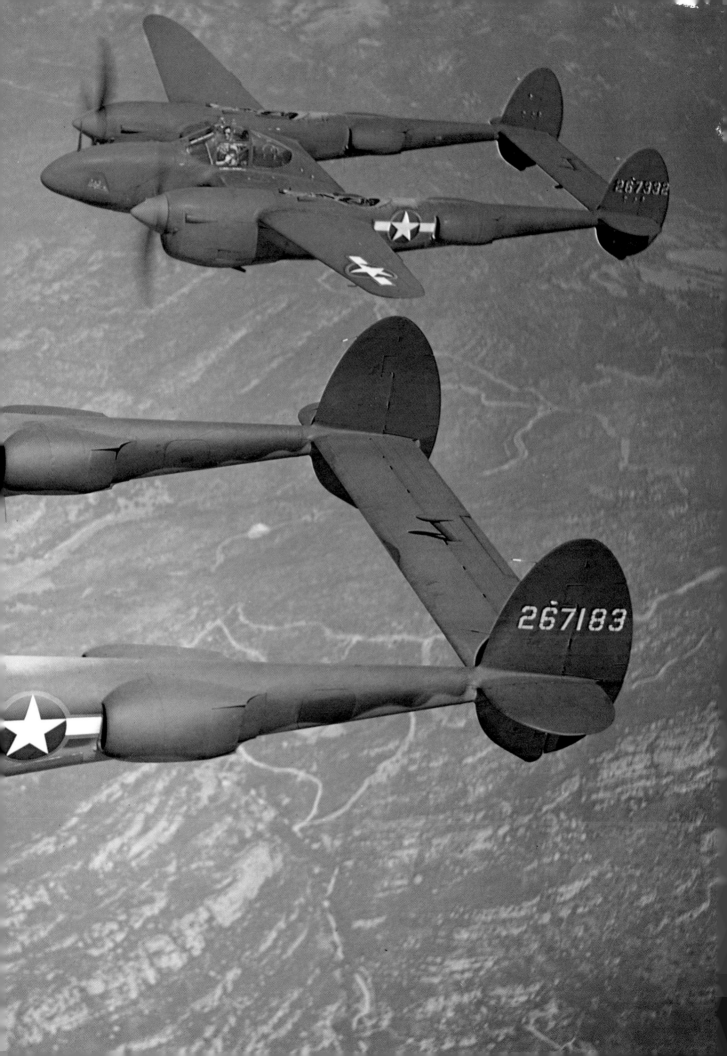

Previous pages: Another radical design, which produced one of the best-known USAAF fighters of World War II, was the twin-boom Lockheed P-38 Lightning.

Below: Britain's second and important turboprop aircraft was the Bristol Britannia, and our illustration shows a BOAC machine crossing the coastline.

Right: In 1952 the de Havilland Comet 1 inaugurated the world's first jet airliner service. Air France were among early users of the type.

(where the wing leading-edge forms an angle of less than 90 degrees to the rear fuselage) reduced buffeting at high speeds. Wind-tunnel tests confirmed this to be true, and also that thin wing sections helped. But no one knew whether it would be possible to design an aircraft able to penetrate safely what newspapers had already dubbed the 'sound barrier'.

In America, the USAF ordered the Bell Aircraft Company to design a robust rocket-powered research aircraft. It was made strong enough to survive, hopefully, the worst buffeting, and powered by a rocket-eingine to give it the necessary speed. Air-launched from beneath a B-29 'mother-plane', its pilot inched it progressively nearer and nearer to the magic figure of Mach 1.0, representing the speed of sound.

Its USAF pilot, Capt. Charles 'Chuck' Yeager, found that at Mach 0.94 the buffeting was so severe it seemed unlikely the little X-1 rocket-plane could survive penetration of this invisible barrier. Finally, on 14 October 1947, Yeager decided he could dally no longer. As he dropped away from the B-29 he slammed the throttle wide open, streaking away into the 'wild blue'.

The little plane began to shudder violently, and 'Chuck' was shaken from side to side as the Mach meter crept nearer to the enigmatic Mach 1. He knew that his control over the aircraft was only marginal: would it, indeed, come against an aerodynamic 'barrier' that would shatter the machine into a thousand pieces?

Suddenly, without any warning, the buffeting stopped completely. A gallant little aircraft and a very brave man had slipped through a chink in the 'barrier' into the smooth airflow of supersonic flight.

While this kind of fundamental research into high speed flight was being pushed ahead all around the world, a new breed of pioneers were seeking to corner the market in fast intercontinental travel. The leader of this revolution was the British de Havilland company, who sought to gain advantage from Britain's lead in turbine-engine technology to produce a world-beating jet airliner.

This emerged as a beautifully proportioned swept-wing configuration known as the Comet 1, its four de Havilland Ghost turbine engines buried neatly within the wing roots. On 2 May 1952 it inaugurated the world's first jet airliner service.

It was an immediate success, and by the time that British Overseas Airways Corporation (BOAC: Imperial Airways' successor) had extended Comet services to Tokyo, in April 1953, de Havilland had accumulated orders for 52 aircraft, including a token order from Pan American which promised exciting prospects.

Then tragedy struck. Two Comets crashed in enexplicable circumstances: when a third was lost the type was grounded immediately. Stranger-than-fiction detection, involving some remarkable salvage work by the Royal Navy, enabled enough of BOAC's *Yoke Peter* (G-ALYP) to be recovered from the sea off Elba for scientists to determine that explosive decompression of the fuselage was responsible for these tragedies.

To enable passengers to breathe normally at heights of up to seven miles (11.3 km), the cabin structure had to be designed to withstand an internal air pressure of 8.25 lb/sq in (0.58 kg/cm^2). Metal fatigue, caused by repeated cycles of pressurization and depressurization, was the villain of the piece.

A sad episode for de Havilland and British aviation, it nevertheless helped aircraft manufacturers of every nation to build new generations of fast, safe airliners.

Britain fortunately had a second string to her bow: the 40-seat Vickers Viscount, powered by the 'turboprop', a more economical variation of the pure jet engine. The gas-driven turbine uses its power, through the medium of reduction gearing, to drive a conventional propeller. Retaining the smooth operation of an engine devoid of reciprocating components, it is considerably more economical in operation than the turbojet.

British European Airways (BEA) Viscounts, first used on the London-Cyprus route on 18 April 1953, were an immediate success. Over 400 were built and, wonder of

Above left: Piston-engined
civil airliners attained the
peak of their development
in such aircraft as the
Lockheed Super Constell-
ation.

Above: At the other end of
the range of piston-engined
aircraft were graceful and
reliable vehicles such as
this Cessna 180, operating
in New Zealand.

Far left: Britain's second
string, after the failure of
the Comet 1, was the Vic-
kers Viscount. It was followed by the more
advanced Vickers Van-
guard illustrated here.

Left: Civil aviation soon
got into high gear after the
end of the World War II.
This interior view of a
Boeing Model 377 Strato-
cruiser gives some idea of
the new luxury travel offered to passengers in what
was then a vast cabin.

wonders, the type even entered service with an American domestic operater, Capitol Airlines.

But while the aircraft designers had been concentrating their efforts on sophisticated airliners for peaceful travel, a new East-West confrontation had come to the boil in Korea. On 25 June 1950 North Korean infantry, spearheaded by Soviet-built tanks, ravaged the 38th Parallel, the invisible barrier separating the Communist-supported North Koreans from the South Koreans, who were to depend increasingly on the United Nations Organization for survival.

Such a conflict was predictable. Since the end of the Berlin Airlift there had an uneasy peace, and it seemed inevitable that the Eastern bloc would endeavour to benefit from the run-down in Allied global military coverage. Observers in the Kremlin were fully aware that conditions in the Far East were ripe for Communist expansion.

Just over three years were to elapse before peace was restored to Korea. During that time new, fast jet fighters were developed and there were the first confrontations between machines like the Russian Mikoyan MiG-15 and America's F-84 Thunderjets and F-86 Sabres.

More significant, perhaps, was the emancipation of the helicopter during this war. The rotary-winged 'chopper', which had made a very brief entry in the closing stages of World War II, soon began to demonstrate its capabilities as a vehicle that could operate into and out of areas inaccessible to any other form of transport and as a field ambulance that reduced the death rate for wounded to the lowest in military history When armed with quite simple weapons it proved to have potential as a close support combat aircraft.

The pioneer airmen of a half-century earlier would have been far happier to know that the helicopter also proved invaluable to rescue rash holidaymakers cut off by tides, egg collectors from cliff faces, amateur yachtsmen from the sea and refugees from floods. They might well have twisted and turned most uncomfortably in their graves if they could have foreseen aviation developments in the next decade.

By the end of the decade the helicopter had already proved an invaluable tool, making survey easy from otherwise inaccesible positions...

... and rescuing people from dangerous situations.

Above: The Douglas A-1
Skyraider was famous in
the US Navy Service, its
availability to carry a wide
range of weapons making
it an invaluable aircraft
during the Korean conflict.

Left: North American
F-86 Sabres were the first
swept-wing fighters to
serve with the USAF. In
the Korean War, opposing
Russian-built Mikoyan
MiG-15s, they recorded
combats between swept-
wing turbojet-powered
fighters.

NEW LOOK FOR AIR TRANSPORT 1954-63

the old order changeth, yielding place to new
Alfred, Lord Tennyson

The uses of such a Chariot (aircraft) may be various); besides the discoveries which might thereby be made in the lunary world; It would be serviceable also for the conveyance of a man to any remote place of this earth: as suppose to the Indies or Antipodes. For when once it was elevated for some few miles, so as to be above that orb of magnetick virtue, which is carried about by earth's diurnal revolution, it might then be very easily and speedily directed to any particular place of this great globe.

It would be one great advantage in this kind of travelling, that one should be perfectly freed from all inconveniences of ways or weather, not having any extremity of heat or cold, or tempests to molest him, this aetherall air being perpetually in an equal temper and calmnesse. The upper parts of the world are always quiet and serene, no winds and blustring there, they are these lower cloudly regions that are so full of tempests and combustion. (John Wilkins, Bishop of Chester, Mathematicall Magick, *1648.)*

It seems hardly possible that any man could have looked ahead so clearly to a period rather more than 300 years in advance of his own time, to a moment when the first great new 'chariots' of the air, in the form of the Boeing 707 and Douglas DC-8, would carry passengers to the 'remote places of this earth', high above the 'lower cloudy regions... so full of tempests'.

Yet at the beginning of this decade, on 15 July 1954, Boeing in America had flown the prototype of a jet-powered tanker/transport designated as the Model 367–80. Soon known by the nickname 'Dash Eighty', it was developed first as a flight refuelling tanker for the USAF. Two years later the company was permitted to develop a civil version, and on 26 October 1958 a Pan American Airways Boeing 707 made the first American jet-powered transatlantic commercial flight.

To Britain had gone the honour of inaugurating the first passenger-carrying jet services over the North Atlantic, on 4 October 1958. This lead of only 22 days shows the extent to which the American aviation industry had made good their time lag on civil jet development. It also speaks volumes for the courage of BOAC, and their faith in the de Havilland Company, leading to production of the Comet 4 which made the initial transatlantic passenger flights. That faith was justified, and Comet 4s are still carrying pas-

sengers, economically and safely, in 1973.

The range of the first model of the Boeing 707, the 707-120, was marginal for the North Atlantic and other long-range routes, but with the emergence of the 707-320 in 1959 this superb aeroplane was soon to be found on airports around the world. In 1972 the 'Dash Eighty', after 18 years' service as a prototype test-bed for the newest brainwaves of Boeing's designers, was presented to the Smithsonian Institution, where it is regarded as one of the twelve most significant aircraft in the history of aviation.

If the new turbojet engines could thrust bigger and better aeroplanes through the air at ever-increasing speeds, of what else were they capable?

Rolls Royce had been giving this some thought, believing they could be used to evolve VTOL (vertical take-off and landing) aircraft quite different from the helicopter. They built a functional test rig that became known as the 'Flying Bedstead', which had two Nene turbojets to provide the lifting thrust. They argued that if the combined thrust of the jet engines was greater than the weight of the test rig it must fly. It did. The development by Bristol Siddeley of what is known as vectored thrust by *Bristol Siddeley*, where the jet exhaust from the engine is passed through rotating nozzles, promised exciting prospects. Such engines in a fixed-wing aircraft should allow vertical take-off on pure jet lift, with gradual transition to horizontal flight as the nozzles rotate, until the forward speed of the aircraft is sufficient for the fixed-wing to support it in conventional flight. The promise was to be realized at a later date.

This was a decade when new ideas and new aircraft were multiplying at an amazing speed. Britain's Fairey Aviation Company built and flew the world's first VTOL airliner. It had monoplane wings, turboprop engines and a large rotor. Compressed-air jets at the rotor tips lifted the craft into the air, after which it flew conventionally as a fixed-wing aircraft, the rotor auto-rotating but providing little lift. This 40/48-seat airliner was way ahead of its time, and the company had inadequate finance to continue with its development.

There was little doubt that VTOL aircraft would become of increasing importance, and civil operators began to in-

A Boeing Model 747 jumbo jet in the insignia of JAL. The jumbos have revolutionized air travel in the 70's, especially in the field of package holiday tours. Japan Air Lines has become renowned for its tours to exotic places in the Far East and for its traditional Japanese hospitality.
Inset: British European Airways were the first airline to carry passengers by helicopter. Today its Sikorsky S-61s offer an exciting beginning to a holiday in the Scilly Isles.

Left: Britain led the way also with the world's first VTOL airliner, the Fairey Rotodyne. This took off and landed as a helicopter, but flew conventionally powered by its turboprop engines.

Below left: Developed after the failure of the Comet 1, the later Comet 4 was still in airline service in 1973. By the time it entered service Britain had lost to the Americans her lead in the construction of turbojet airliners.

evolved: the business or executive aircraft, sleek twin-engined machines with six to eight seats.

By the time the aviation industry had geared itself to meet the requirements of an enormous post-war market, there seemed to be little that the aeroplane was not able to do. Aircraft spread fertilisers or insecticides; controlled traffic; made aerial surveys; fought forest fires; tried to produce rain; fed starving cattle; inspected electric cables, pipe lines and fence-lines; carried the sick to hospital; relieved lighthouse keepers; counted animal populations; and restocked over-fished lakes. The list is almost endless.

This was all a part of the dreams of the pioneers: But sinister developments of the aviation industry were infiltrating this bright scene. It should not be forgotten that World War II had produced practical examples of four significant devices: the helicopter, turbojet engine, guided missile and atomic bomb. Marriage of the first two, favoured on all sides, considerably enhanced the potential of rotary-winged aircraft.

A union between the second pair could hardly be regarded without horror. But because it promised the realization of an ultimate weapon there were those who were anxious for the wedding day and fruits of matrimony.

Anyone with a broad view of the aviation scene when the war in Europe came to its end in the flaming ruins of Berlin, soon realized the kind of weapons that could evolve from the V2 rocket. Consequently, both East and West scrambled to acquire the benefits of German research, using as many of their scientists as could be induced to start a new life in the country of a former enemy, and all available stocks of V-weapons for test purposes.

America gained the services of Wernher von Braun. Soon after becoming established in the United States he was made leader of a team of scientists and engineers at the Army's Redstone Arsenal, in Alabama. Long before this, of course, war in Japan had ended with the first mushroom clouds of nuclear warfare over Hiroshima and Nagasaki. The scene was set for a 'shotgun' wedding of the rocket and atomic bomb.

Realization of a guided missile was comparatively easy. Far more difficult was the creation of an atomic war-head; the first nuclear bombs had been big, clumsy weapons. Something far more advanced was needed to fit within the streamlined confines of a rocket. Strangely, American skill at developing a small but potent nuclear weapon was initially to be a disadvantage. The Soviet Union, then unable to evolve a small atomic warhead, concentrated on the design of large booster rockets able to lift the heavier warhead.

The first product of von Braun's team was called Redstone. It was a ballistic missile with interchangeable high-

vestigate the potential of the helicopter for passenger carrying. To British European Airways had gone the honour of operating the first helicopter passenger service; but the Belgian airline Sabena had inaugurated the first international helicopter network and had carried more than 100,000 passengers by mid-1957.

In America there was an almost explosive growth in private flying. She emerged from the war with enormous production capacity in all kinds of industries, which bent their efforts to filling the vacuum for consumer goods, in the process creating a financial boom. The North American continent was ideal for the growth of private aviation: a good climate, cheap fuel, lots of space and people with money to spend.

The 'big three' of light plane production, Beech, Cessna and Piper, turned out large numbers of beautifully finished lightweight cabin monoplanes, and experienced designers began to produce plans of aircraft that could be built by amateur constructors. Some of the amateurs even evolved original designs for homebuilt aircraft: in general the standard of their workmanship was high.

With American businessmen and salesmen anxious to travel quickly over long distances to speed the marketing of their company's products, a whole new line of aircraft

Below: Around the world
specialized aircraft demon-
trated that they were able
to serve man for peaceful
purposes, such as carrying
the sick to hospital from a
Scottish island's tide-
washed airstrip.

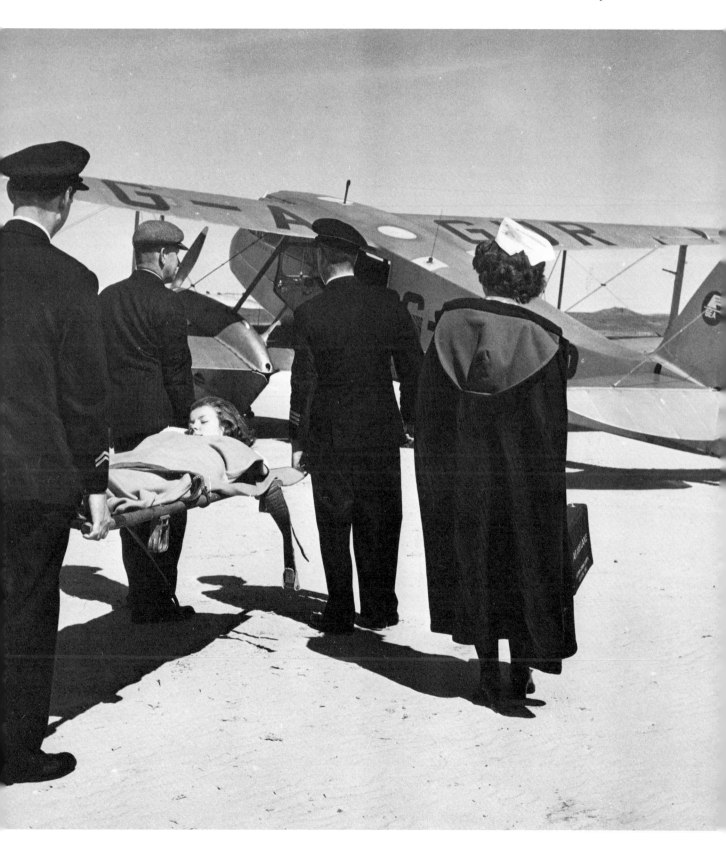

Left: Fire-fighting is one of the valuable services offered by aircraft. This Canadair CL-215 'water bomber' is in use with the Service de la Protection Civile de France.

Right: With the failure of President Dwight D. Eisenhower's 'open skies' policy, the Lockheed U-2 reconnaissance aircraft had an important part to play in the East-West balance of power.

Below right: As the world's air forces became equipped with turbine-powered aircraft, jet-powered trainers assumed considerable importance. This Canadair CL-41G multirole training /tactical aircraft is seen in the insignia of the Royal Malaysian Air Force.

Left: Before man could travel in space, he needed to gain experience of weightlessness. Soviet cosmonauts seen training in a transport aircraft which is flying in a free-fall trajectory, providing a short period of zero-gravity.

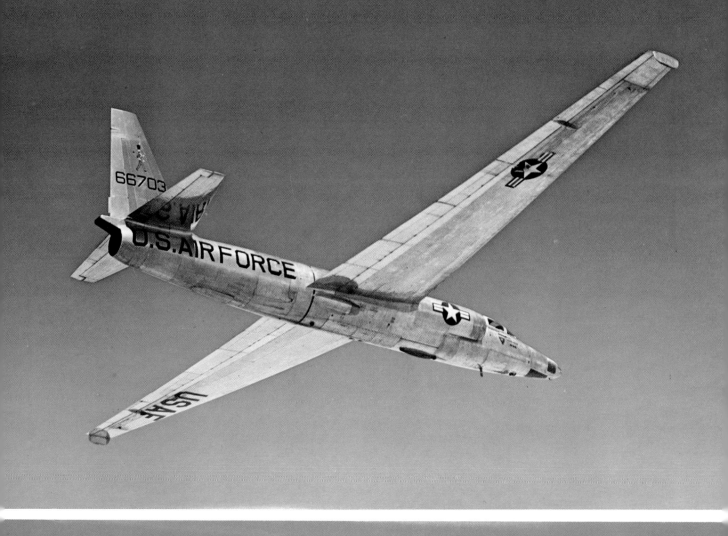

explosive or nuclear warheads, which first became operational in 1956. Almost inevitably it was an enlarged version of the German V2, but by 1957 this weapon was developed to give a range of 1,500 miles (2,414 km).

If the military faction prime interest in the rocket was further travelling and more destructive missiles, it had a quite different appeal for scientists. Even before the Wright brothers' achievement of powered flight in 1903, Konstantin Eduardovitch Tsiolkovsky in Russia had prorounded the use of liquid propellants for rockets, and in 1903 had defined the form of a rocket-powered spacecraft. Today regarded as the 'father of space flight', he was the first to realize that a multi-stage rocket would be needed to escape from earth's gravitational pull. He suggested that as the propellants of each stage were consumed it should be made to fall away, thus reducing the weight to be accelerated to escape velocity.

His theoretical work was expanded by R. Esnault-Pelterie of France, but the first serious experimental scientists were Robert H. Goddard in America and Hermann Oberth of Austria. Their dream was the dream which had first led von Braun to join the VfR in Germany: space and interplanetary travel.

With improving rocket technology, American scientists and engineers planned to put a small satellite into earth orbit during the 1957 International Geophysical Year. The most advanced project was the Vanguard, but before its first launch news came from Russia, on 4 October 1957, that a 184 lb (83 kg) satellite, Sputnik 1, was bleeping its way round the world. This was a great achievement and the Americans, despite their disappointment at being forestalled, were among the first to offer hearty congratulations to the Soviet scientists.

When Vanguard's initial launch 19 days later was considered highly successful, it seemed certain that America's first artificial satellite would not be far behind Sputnik 1. Unfortunately, the next two Vanguard launchings were complete failures.

Even more devastating was the news, which came on 3 November 1957, that a satellite, Sputnik 2, was circling the world carrying a dog named Laika, the first living creature to travel in space. Great was the concern of animal lovers when Laika was painlessly put to death eight days later. No one then knew how to recover a satellite from orbit.

Right: Fish and water stream from the belly of a specially-adapted agricultural aircraft as an Australian lake is restocked with yearling trout.

Below right: Millions of acres of valuable timberland in America and Canada have been saved by the combined efforts of fire-fighting smoke-jumpers who descend by parachute, hose-carrying helicopters and water-bombers.

Far right: Top dressing with fertilizers, often a hazardous task for the pilot, has become an important part of the agricultural scene.

But for American scientists, and more especially her military planners, the most staggering piece of information was that Sputnik 2 weighed nearly half a ton. The implication was that the Soviet Union must possess booster rockets of great power. The big question was: how advanced are her military rockets?

It was something of an anti-climax when, on 31 January 1958, the Americans succeeded in getting an 18 lb (8.2 kg) satellite into orbit. But thanks to American advances in miniaturized equipment, this little piece of iron mongery, known as 'Explorer 1', achieved a great deal and more than lived up to its name.

Transmissions of data by Sputnik 2 had suggested that future travellers in space need have little fear of cosmic or solar radiation. Quite different was the story unfolded by Explorer 1, for Geiger tubes placed on board were deluged by radiation. Subsequently, other Explorers provided confirmation that a huge belt of radiation – to become known as the Van Allen belt – surrounded the earth. This belt runs parallel to the equator, with relatively clear areas above the North and South Poles.

As East and West made their respective announcements of new success in space exploration, the newspapers began to speak of a 'space race'. Of far greater concern to America, whose post-war affluence had elected her as primary peace-keeper of the Western world, was the knowledge that Russia then held a lead in space capability: it had to be assumed that the Russians held a similar development lead in rockets for military purposes. To add to the gravity of the situation, Russia had detonated its first atomic bomb in 1949. The danger of an all-out nuclear war was clear, and the most frightening aspect was that it could be initiated by a trigger-happy individual.

The American President, Dwight D. Eisenhower, had attempted to eliminate this situation in July 1955, when he had proposed at a summit conference in Geneva what he termed an 'open skies' policy. Briefly, it called for an East-West exchange of military information, arms limitation, and mutual facilities for aerial reconnaissance so that both nations should be constantly aware of the military potential of the other. Pre-knowledge of any arms build-up could overcome the danger of surprise attack.

This proposal came too early: the Soviets were not prepared to share with anyone the secrets of their increasing nuclear capability. The only policy that could be adopted by the West was vast expenditure to ensure the availability of annihilating nuclear weapons that would have sufficient deterrent power to make a nuclear war unthinkable.

Thus was born the 'cold war', with both sides involved in an arms race, adding to their inventories the most horrifying weapons ever created by Man. The civilian masses of the world realized that the far-fetched ideas of science fiction writers had become reality, and that unless the sanity of civilization could prevail, the world might be destroyed in a holocaust of nuclear war.

Ethical or not, America was convinced that clandestine reconnaissance was necessary to maintain a full knowledge of developments in the East. This led to the creation of an amazing aeroplane by C.L. ('Kelly') Johnson of the Lockheed Company. Known as the U-2, this remarkable aircraft could fly so high there seemed little likelihood of it being intercepted, and possessed a long-range capability that would enable it to overfly the vast areas of Soviet territory. So that its reconnaissance sorties would be all-revealing, Dr Edwin Land had developed for it a remarkable camera capable of pinpointing golf balls on a putting green 55,000 ft (16,800 m) below the aircraft's track.

This revolutionary aeroplane, in July 1955, first gave the true story of an event which staggered those who witnessed the Soviet Aviation Day fly-past over Moscow. To the amazement of spectators, squadron after squadron of heavy bombers passed in review overhead. Their numbers seemed endless, and far exceeded the estimates prepared by Western military intelligence.

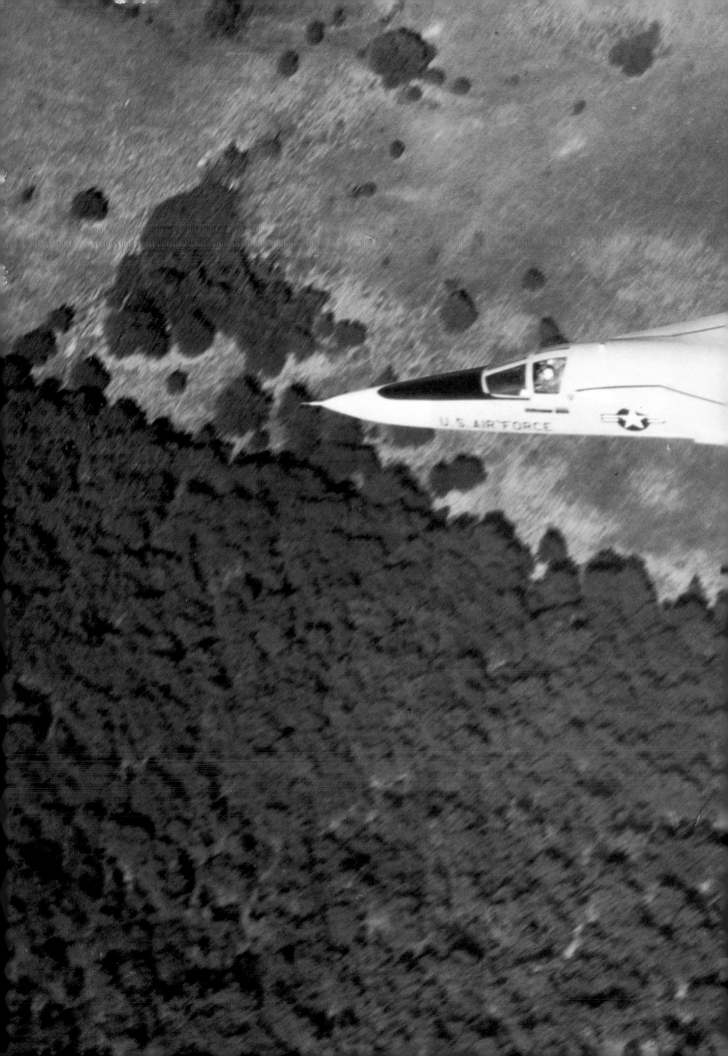

Previous pages: First flown at Fort Worth, Texas, on 21 December 1964, the General Dynamics F-111A variable-geometry two-seat tactical fighter/bomber. Despite controversial entry into service, it was to prove an important tactical weapon at the closing stages of the Vietnam War.

Above: Vanguard II atop its rocket launcher, a mere 20 in. (0.51 m) diameter satellite, typical of an early space probe.

Above: Most important of America's early space research rockets was Explorer 1, launched from Cape Canaveral on 31 January 1958, which gave confirmation that the earth was surrounded by huge belts of radiation.

Right: On 12 April 1961 the world was electrified by the news that a man was encircling earth, orbiting in space. Russia's Vostok 1 spacecraft, attached to its cylindrical instrument section, which had carried Yuri Gagarin into the immortality of history.

Amazement turned to serious concern as the potential of this vast air armada became apparent. But the U-2 revealed that it was a hoax, a circle of comparatively few bombers gyrating over the review area. In fact, Russia had been concentrating on the creation of new long-range ballistic missiles in great numbers while the nations of the West remained fairly happy in the belief that she had been building up a moderately large conventional force of aircraft.

It was not until 1960, when the Soviet Union electrified the world with the news that Francis Gary Powers was held in Lubyanka Prison, Moscow, that ordinary men and women learned of the destruction by a ground-to-air missile of this amazing aircraft. For the first time they heard the designation U-2 mentioned as claims and counter-claims boiled up between East and West. The Russians sought to gain maximum publicity from these 'spy-plane' operations, and claimed they were aggressive provocation, when Powers was put on public trial in Moscow on 17 August 1960, more than three months after his capture.

Powers' position was indefensible: much of the aircraft and its equipment had been recovered and it was so deep in Soviet territory that no plea of being off-course would have been credible. After two days' trial he was sentenced to ten years imprisonment. Happily, a fortuitous exchange for the Soviet spy, Col. Rudolf Abel, meant that he served only twenty months of this term before returning to America.

As is inevitable in a case of this kind, many in the West were critical of such activities. There were those who suggested that such acts carried out by America were warming-up rather than cooling-off the tension between East and West. One must conjecture the feelings of those critics when, two years later, the U-2 played a vital role in preventing the outbreak of what could have escalated so easily into a third world war.

The establishment of a left-wing regime in Cuba in 1953, under Fidel Castro, had brought close links with the Soviet Union. Routine reconnaissance over Cuba was considered a prudent precaution and during one of these, on 29 August 1962, photographs taken by a U-2 revealed the establishment of surface-to-air missile (SAM) sites on the island. Although a closer look confirmed they were of Russian origin, their defensive rather than offensive role caused no great concern in American military circles. It was decided, however, to keep a sharp eye on any other developments.

Almost two months passed without great excitement, by which time the whole of the island had been well photographed. All seemed innocent, until a photo-interpreter with experience of military installations in Russia noted that deployment of SAM sites near the town of San Cristobal was in a pattern used by the Soviets to protect missile bases.

His careful study of the photographs demanded more intense reconnaissance, and by 21 October there was no doubt that medium-range ballistic missiles were being installed on launchers that were trained against the industrial area of north-east America. In the United States hotseat at that time was President John F. Kennedy who, in his inaugural address only 21 months earlier, had said: '...only a few generations have been granted the role of defending freedom in its hour of maximum danger. I do not shrink from this responsibility...'

Though that moment had arrived long before President Kennedy might have expected, he acted immediately and calmly. He marshalled the tremendous offensive power of the American forces, simultaneously despatching couriers to Britain, France and West Germany with photographic evidence of the situation on Cuba.

On 22 October 1962, in a now historic broadcast, he let the Soviet Union know that America would pay any price to preserve peace; that they would '...regard any nuclear missile launched from Cuba against any nation in the western hemisphere as an attack by the Soviet Union on the United States, requiring a full retaliatory response upon the Soviet Union...' They were stern words for a grave situation, and ordinary men and women of all nationalities waited anxiously: was this the Armageddon of the Book of Revelation?

It was a long, tense wait, nearly triggered into explosion on 27 October when a U-2, making a routine check of the Cuban missile sites, was destroyed by a SAM. Kennedy played it cool, ordering his forces to instant readiness for massive retaliation if this was, in fact, the first shot of War.

Above left: Lockheed produced their L-1011 Tri-Star, but it was beaten into service by the McDonnell Douglas DC-10 wide-bodied jet airliner.

Above: Eventually regarded as one of the 12 most significant aircraft in aviation history, the Boeing Model 707 prototype during an early test flight.

Left: In Europe an international consortium of aero-space manufacturers, representing France, Germany, the Netherlands, Spain and the United Kingdom, have built the short-medium range wide-bodied transport known as the Airbus A-300B, due to enter service in 1974.

Below: Looking rather like a highly-decorated hot-air balloon of the Montgolfier era, this 170 lb (77 kg) satellite, Telstar, first gave a hint of the potential round-the-world television communication.

Right: America put her first man into suborbital space flight when astronaut Alan B. Shepard was carried in the Mercury capsule *Freedom 7*, 302 miles (486 km) down the Atlantic Missile Range.

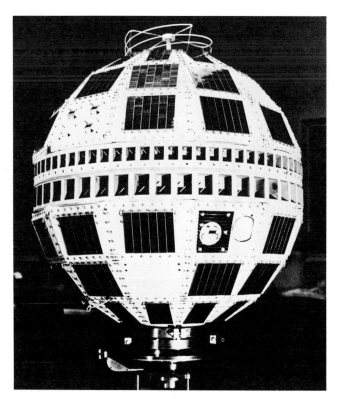

The conclusion for which the world had prayed came on the following morning, when Premier Krushchev announced that the missile sites on Cuba would be dismantled and the weapons returned to Russia. The aeroplane, which had been conceived originally for peaceful purposes, and the camera, a device invented to record the beautiful things of our world, had combined to give a little more breathing space for the rationalizing processes of civilization.

While this aggressive development of the V2 rocket had been taking place, there had been no relaxation of the activities of the scientists and engineers who dedicated their efforts to peaceful travel in space. In America and Russia the primary target was the moon, and when on 31 January 1961 a Mercury spacecraft carrying a chimpanzee was launched successfully in ballistic flight down the US Atlantic Missile Range, it was believed that significant progress had been made towards the realization of man in space.

Less than three months later America was to receive an electrifying shock when it learned that a Soviet spacecraft, Vostock 1, had carried Russia's Maj. Yuri Gagarin for a single orbit of the earth on 12 April 1961. Landing safely 1 hr 48 min. after launch, Gagarin's name is recorded illegibly in the history of astronautics, the first man in the world to be orbited in space. Tragically, this brave man was killed in a flying accident on 28 March 1968.

The next success was also Russian. Cosmonaut Herman Titov was launched in Vostok 2, on 6 August 1961, to record 17 orbits before a safe landing the following day. Not until 20 February 1962 were the people of America thrilled by the successful three-orbit flight of astronaut John Glenn of the US Marine Corps, in the Mercury spacecraft Friendship.

This acclimatization of man to travel in space and the rendezvous, docking and space walk activities that were to occupy several years, were all part of the techniques that must be learned before any attempt could be made to put a man on the moon.

Before that was even remotely possible it was necessary to learn a great deal about our nearest neighbour in space which seems so near near us when close to the horizon in its full phase. The moon's nearness is illusory, for its orbit is elliptical and the distance which separates it from earth varies between 225,740 miles (363,298 km) and 251,967 miles (405,505 km).

Only one face of the moon was known to astronomers. Would the hidden side offer a better landing site: was its surface deep in lunar dust that would bury a spacecraft attempting to land? These are but two of the innumerable questions to which answers were needed.

Russia made the first physical contact with the moon on 14 September 1959, when her Luna 2 spacecraft crashed onto the surface. In the following month, after launch on 4 October, Luna 3 provided, by television link, Man's first view of the hidden side of the lunar surface: it proved to be the limit of man's successful exploration of the moon in this decade.

If the 'man in the street' could see little sense in the astronomical expenditure on space programmes intended to put man on the moon, he was at least thrilled by the potential of a communications satellite called Telstar 1. Launched on 10 July 1962 this meant that for the first time in history, Americans and Europeans watching television screens in the comfort of their own homes could see events taking place on both sides of the Atlantic.

Telstar 1 was followed by Relay 1 on 13 December 1962 and Telstar 2 on 13 May 1963, allowing more frequent television transmissions of current events. As the decade neared its end, life seemed a little more peaceful; some people believed that the intensity of the moon-fever gripping America and Russia could lead to a new understanding between nations. They might have felt more concerned had they been aware that, just before Christmas, transport aircraft of the US Pacific Air Force had dropped by parachute 4½ tons of Christmas provender for Special Forces personnel stationed in isolated areas of Vietnam.

Left: This very colourful DHC-6 Twin Otter, built by de Havilland Aircraft of Canada, offers third-level airline operators the capability of serving communities whose airports are little more than convenient meadows.

Below: A glimpse of the future? The Anglo-French Concorde supersonic transport as it may well appear on airports around the world if it enters service in 1974.

Below: Russia's supersonic transport, the Tupolev Tu-144, with nose drooped and 'moustache' foreplanes extended, looks rather like a strange insect, surrounded by admiring crowds at the 1973 Paris Air Show.

Right (top): The Boeing Model 707, which first entered airline service in 1958, is still being sold to new customers in 1973.

Right (bottom): In Russia the Tupolev Tu-134, typical of modern medium-range turbojet transports with rear-mounted engines, is in service with Aeroflot and many other Eastern airlines.

INCREDIBLE
DECADE
1964-73

Think about flying around in daylight and good weather only 200 feet above the ground and going up and down over hills and into valleys, keeping this height.

The speaker is Capt. Jackie Crouch of one of the USAF's Tactical Fighter Wings who, in the closing stages of the Vietnam War, was pilot of a General Dynamics F-111A 'swing-wing' tactical fighter/bomber.

Now do this at night, in mountains and in heavy cloud when you can't see anything outside the cockpit. That is really, really exciting, even without the enemy threat.

It takes real discipline to come up over these mountains, as we did at night, out on top of the cloud layer in the moonlight. We'd see those jagged peaks all around us poking through the cloud tops, and we'd have to put the nose down back into that mist. And as we went down the moonlight would fade, and the clouds get darker, and we'd know we were descending below those peaks and were depending on our radars and our autopilots—and with Hanoi coming up . . .

I won't say that I wasn't worried.

One night when the weather was very bad, I was in cloud for the last eleven minutes before bombs away—and that means at the lowest levels of the whole flight, going up and down fully and keeping our clearance still at 200 to 250 feet above these obstructions.

We didn't see a thing outside the cockpit, not even after the bombs left us. For me this was really remarkable. Even now I can't explain how fantastic it was . . .

Not many years ago that would have been pure science fiction, which one would have read excitedly but with disbelief. Now, in our present-day technological world, nothing seems to surprise us.

The F-111A was, perhaps, one of the most controversial aircraft ever to enter service with the USAF, as revolutionary as the British TSR.2 axed by the Labour government of Harold Wilson. Its development began in the late 1950s to meet the USAF's requirement for an aeroplane that could operate into and out of short and rough fields, have supersonic speed at low level, and better Mach 2 for combat at altitude, coupled with Atlantic or Pacific ferry range capability.

To meet the wide diversity in speeds, a variable-geometry wing was adopted. This gives it a fairly normal-looking wing to provide maximum life in slow-speed flight, which can be swept back so that the aircraft's high-speed configuration becomes more like that of a paper dart. Two powerful turbofan engines enable it to haul an incredible total of over 30,000 lb (13,608 kg) of mixed ordnance, which amounts to something more than the combined weight of five Battle of Britain Mk.1 Spitfires.

So that the 'plane and its two-man crew can get in low, below the enemy's defensive radar, in all weathers by day or night, it is equipped with terrain-following radar (TFR) linked to autopilots. This explains the 'science fiction' mountain-hugging performance related by Jackie Crouch at the beginning of the chapter.

When six F-111As were sent into Southeast Asia for combat evaluation in March 1968 three were lost in the first four weeks, causing an outcry in Congress. But there was nothing

wrong with the fundamental design of the aeroplane, as later events were to prove.

At the end of 1963 the Americans had not been directly involved in a shooting war in Vietnam. Instead, they had large numbers of service specialists in the country to advise the South Vietnamese on building up resistance against the infiltration of the Viet Cong from the North, who were aided and inspired by their Communist allies in Russia and China. There was no change until the Tonking Gulf incident, on 2 August 1964, when units of the US Seventh Fleet, cruising outside the 12-mile (19-km) limit off the North Vietnam coast, were attacked by motor torpedo-boats of Russian design. Immediately, the US changed her role from advice to participation, because clearly this was another case of potential Communist expansion. It was a conflict which was to continue almost to the end of this decade.

This was a new kind of warfare, quite unlike the two great world wars in which vast armies had been in direct confrontation. Instead, it was a deadly game of hide-and-seek, with air power given the task of finding the infiltrators and guerrillas, and then striking to eliminate them before they could disperse into the all-enveloping jungle.

New techniques were evolved to deal with the situation and a primary role was that of the forward air controllers (FACs). Rather like policeman on a beat, each had his own area of patrol and, at the first sign of suspicious movement, called in strike aircraft to deluge marked areas with bombs, napalm or vicious fire from rockets and guns. When it was realized that this strike role was imposing a great strain on primary combat aircraft, older types like the famed Douglas C-47 (Dakota) of World War II re-entered service in a combat role. Equipped as heavily-armed gunships, they could put down a deadly hail of fire when called in by the FACs.

This enabled the fast, hard-striking combat aircraft to be deployed more regularly in a strategic role, striking at airfields, transport routes and SAM sites in Viet Cong territory. They were backed up by the might of the Boeing B-52 Stratofortresses of Strategic Air Command, which pounded industrial targets in North Vietnam with a massive weight of high-explosive bombs.

Rotary-winged aircraft evolved as important weapons in a constantly widening field. They had proved their value in Korea, putting down troops and evacuating casualties from otherwise inaccessible positions. The more powerful helicopters that were now available were used in Vietnam to transport heavy weapons and recover aircraft shot down by the enemy, while more agile versions rescued their aircrew. Most significant was the development of heavily-armed combat helicopters, equipped with rapid-firing cannon or grenade launchers, that were able to scatter an enemy with salvoes of rockets. Allied to the typical flight characteristics of a 'chopper', these features have made them valuable close-support aircraft.

The constant search for small units of infiltrators gave new impetus to the development of reconnaissance and surveillance aircraft. Cameras alone were inadequate for the task, and once-sleek aircraft developed strange bumps and protrusions which housed advanced sensors designed to help find the needle in the jungle haystack. Infra-red devices to detect the heat emission from the exhaust of enemy vehicles, electronic 'eyes' to 'see' in the dark, and even 'people sniffers' to pick up the smells exuded by human bodies.

Involved, yet again, in a war taking place on the other side of the world, the USAF were spurred by the enormous logistics task to procure huge transport aircraft such as the Lockheed C-141 Star Lifter and C-5A Galaxy. As well as bringing in troops, equipment, supplies and ammunition, they could also be used for casualty evacuation. Even special aircraft for aeromedical evacuation of serious casualties have evolved, such as the McDonnell Douglas C-9A Nightingale, which has included an intensive-care compartment in its special interior.

One other aspect of air power in this conflict deserves mention. 'Drone' aircraft, flown under remote control by radio, have long been used by air forces as airborne targets to train anti-aircraft gunners: and heaven help the poor individual that destroyed one. New developments in avionics have made far more sophisticated drones possible. Known as remotely piloted vehicles (RPVs), and equipped with cameras and/or sensors, they can be air-launched from a 'mother plane' and sent on reconnaissance sorties considered too hazardous for manned aircraft. Their mission completed, they return to rendezvous with a specially-equipped helicopter which retrieves them in the air and carries them back to base. It is not bordering on science fiction to suggest that RPVs may soon be capable of terrain-following offensive missions like those of the F-111As which opened this chapter.

Eight-and-a-half years of commitment in Vietnam, until the cease-fire agreement of early 1973, imposed immense pressures on the United States. There has been also the continuing problem of global strategy concerned with the maintenance of adequate deterrent power to preserve peace: peace through fear. Even this is desirable in preference to the potential of a third world war which, although it might be conventional in origin, could so easily become a nuclear holocaust.

East and West have spent umpteen kings' ransoms to develop their inventories of intercontinental ballistic missiles (ICMBs) housed in silos beneath the ground or submarines in the oceans' depths. Like Pandora's box they wait to release their evils upon our world. Already programmed for their potential targets, they need little more than the pressure of a finger on a button to send them on their journey of destruction.

When the German V2s were first launched against Allied targets, no defence was possible. Only attack upon their point of origin could prevent them from being fired. Now, anti-missile missiles exist, supposedly capable of dealing with incoming multiple independently-targeted warheads. And as if that was not enough, in late 1967 the US Secretary of Defense said that Russia appeared to be developing a space bomb. Called a Fractional Orbital Bombardment System (FOBS), it was envisaged as a weapon in earth orbit which could be caused to fall on a pre-determined target.

To keep an eye on such developments it has been necessary to design and construct spy satellites to supplement the information acquired by more conventional reconnaissance aircraft. We have completed the circle back to the situation which existed early in World War I, when the combatants had to find weapons to destroy the reconnaissance aircraft of the opposing nation. There seems little doubt that both America and Russia already have such a capability. Why don't they use it? The answer at first was that neither could afford to lose the vital reconnaissance role provided by their 'eyes' in space—which would soon happen if either destroyed one or all of the other's satellites. 'Forewarned is forearmed' is as true now as when the words were first uttered.

Are we, then, committed to perpetual and ever-mounting defence expenditure so that we can live in 'peace' to earn the money to pay for continued peace? It is too early to give a reasoned answer to this question. Two-and-a-half years of Strategic Arms Limitation Talks (SALT) preceded signature of the SALT agreement between America and Russia in May 1972, and only time will tell whether this is effective in creating a better understanding and a reduction of tension between East and West. If nothing else, it has made the reconnaissance satellite 'respectable', for both sides agreed they must be allowed to 'see' that the game was being played according to the rules.

Enough of war. What about aviation for peace in this seventh decade of powered flight?

There is little doubt that the aeroplane has changed the whole pattern of world transport. In early 1970 the British passenger liner SS *Empress of England* was offered for sale, because 'competition from air traffic was making its operation uneconomic'. In other words, most passengers between points A and B still want the fastest means of travel.

This line of thought in America, Britain, France and Russia, suggested that a supersonic transport (SST) aircraft, which could halve block times on long-distance routes,

would have great appeal to the intercontinental passenger. Lack of funds, however, prevented development of America's Boeing 2707–300.

Britain and France joined forces, and construction of two prototype Concordes began in 1965. First to fly, on 2 March 1969, was the French-assembled 001 (F-WTSS), followed by the British-assembled 002 (G-BSST) just over a month later, on 9 April. By the end of July 1973 the two prototypes and two pre-production Concordes had accumulated some 2,000 flying hours between them. This figure will be almost doubled before the first Concorde enters airline service, if it does, in 1974. It will be one of the most tested airlines in civil aviation's history.

Russia has 'gone it alone', and the prototype Tu-144 (CCCP-68001) produced by the Tupolev design team beat Concorde into the air, flying for the first time on 31 December 1968. Generally similar in configuration to the Anglo-French SST 'Concordski', as it has been nicknamed in the West, is expected to enter service with the national airline Aeroflot during 1975. Tragically, an improved pre-production version (CCCP-77102) crashed during a flight demonstration at the 1973 Paris Air Show. It was a major disaster, similar to that suffered by the Comet 1. The Tupolev design team must be congratulated for the fact that, like de Havilland before them, they have sufficient confidence in the basic design philosophy to press on with development and certification of the type. Their courage is perhaps even greater, when one considers the immense costs involved; there can be few people who do not wish them every success.

The decade has also seen the introduction of the new generation of wide-bodied jet airliners into worldwide ser-

vice. First of these to fly was the superb Boeing Model 747, quickly tagged with the name 'Jumbo-jet'. That was hardly surprising, for everything connected with it is jumbo-sized. Maximum take-off weight of the 747-200B is over 340 tons, and its 51,000 US gallons (193031 litre) fuel capacity would be enough to power an average family motor car for over a million miles. Basic accommodation is for 382 passengers, but alternative economy-class seating will allow for up to 500. Pan American inaugurated transatlantic services on 22 January 1970, and the 'Jumbo' has continued to provide the major airlines of the Western world with fast and safe travel.

The 747 was followed into service by the 255/380-seat McDonnell Douglas DC-10 on 5 August 1971, and Lockheed's 256/400-seat L-1011 TriStar on 26 April 1972. In Europe, an international consortium is developing a short or medium-range wide-bodied transport, the Airbus A-300B, the first of which is due to enter service in 1974.

In the class of more conventional airliners there are many offering high standards of performance and safety. The Boeing 707, which first entered service in 1958, is still an important part of the aviation scene, as are the Boeing Models 727 and 737 and the McDonnell Douglas DC-8 and DC-9. Britain has contributed the BAC VC-10, One-Eleven and Hawker Siddeley Trident, France the Caravelle, Russia the IL-62 and Tupolev Tu-134 and Tu-154, to name only the major types.

There are also a large number of short-haul airliners produced by manufacturers all over the world, and smaller aircraft for third-level and feeder airlines, as well as some extravagantly-equipped de luxe executive aircraft.

In the field of private flying, especially in America and Europe, the number of lightweight types grows annually. Several kinds of rotary-wing aircraft have entered this field. But in military and civil use the ubiquitous helicopter improves constantly in capability and reliability; its importance in maintaining crews of off-shore drilling rigs involved in the search for new sources of natural gas and oil increases.

Specialized cargo aircraft range from the grotesque Aero Spacelines Guppy-201, which can carry large booster rocket stages and major aircraft assemblies, to little lightweight machines like Cessna's one/six-seat Stationair cargo/utility version with capacity for 101.2 cu ft (2.87 m³) of cargo.

On the military scene there is a steady proliferation of new types of aircraft to meet changing strategy. There is not enough space to catalogue them here. It is pertinent, however, to mention the emphasis on development of armed helicopters, lightweight, highly manoeuvrable fighters, and advanced reconnaissance and surveillance aircraft. Of particular interest in this latter category must be the US Navy's Lockheed S-3A Viking and the British Hawker Siddeley HS

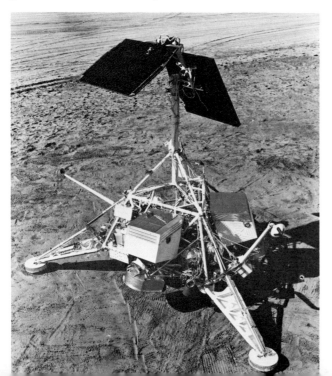

Left: A view of Apollo Command and Service modules in moon orbit, as seen from the Lunar Module.

Right: The desolation of the moon's surface is typified in this shot which shows astronaut Harrison Schmitt working alongside the Lunar roving vehicle during the final Apollo 17 mission.

801 Nimrod for the RAF's Strike Command. Anti-submarine warfare (ASW) has attained prime importance since the development of nuclear-powered missile-launching submarines, which at the time of their introduction into operational service were regarded as the ultimate weapon. Both the above-mentioned aircraft are marvels of electronic equipment, with the sole purpose of hunting and killing enemy submarines anywhere in the world's seas, should the occasion arise.

We have come back to the war theme. Let us look instead into space. In 1963, America and Russia were both capable of launching and retrieving manned spacecraft from earth-orbit, and were taking their first close-up looks at the moon by means of rocket probes.

America's Ranger spacecraft were the first to provide detailed pictures of the lunar surface, transmitting continuously as they approached and eventually crashed on the moon. Ranger 9 will be the best remembered, because its transmissions were relayed on public television circuits. Few who saw those exciting pictures will forget the first close-up glimpse of the cratered and mountainous surface. It seemed an inhospitable environment for man after a quarter-million mile journey – if such a journey were ever possible. And what of the return?

Ranger was succeeded by a series of Lunar Orbiters which during 1966/67 photographed almost the entire surface of the moon. But Russia achieved the next vital step, on 3 February 1966, when Luna 9 soft-landed on the surface. This was the first move in proving whether the environment would allow man to make such a hazardous journey. It was soon clear that it was a practical possibility for a spacecraft to land on the moon and take off again.

Television was to provide earth-bound viewers with an unexpected thrill on Christmas Eve 1968, when Apollo 9 carried astronauts Frank Borman, James Lovell and William Anders in orbit 70 miles (113 km) above the lunar surface. For the first time in history we were able to gaze at the fantastic picture of our own world seen from outer space, floating serenely like another, but more colourful, moon. This sight, more than anything else, must have brought some appreciation of the reason why man is urged on constantly to explore: even into the alien atmosphere of worlds beyond his world.

Once again it was television which brought *the* picture-memory of a lifetime, that of the lunar module *Eagle* carrying Neil Armstrong and Edwin Aldrin to man's first landing on the moon, at 21.18 BST on 20 July 1969. This first mission was crowned with success when the command module splashed down safely on 24 July.

Since then we have had the drama of Apollo 13, signalled first by astronaut Jack Swigert's announcement, electrifying mission control and the world with the understatement of this, or any other, decade: 'Hey, we've got a problem here.' Indeed they had. Courageous, skilled, and hard teamwork, on earth and in space, brought the crew safely back home on 17 April 1970, witnessed by what was then estimated to be the largest television audience in history. Since then we have seen the completion of the Apollo programme, which ended with the Apollo 17 mission. The last three were made more effective by the availability of the Boeing Lunar Roving Vehicle, which allowed surface exploration at a radius of up to about six miles (9.6 km) from the lunar module.

Russia's exploration of the moon has not, so far, involved putting men on the surface. She has achieved brilliant success in two quite different ways: firstly, by her automatic spacecraft Luna 16 and 20, which made soft-landings on the surface and took soil samples by means of a rotary-percussion drill. The samples were then transferred automatically to the recovery capsule before they were blasted off to begin the long journey back to earth. Secondly, they have carried two Lunokhod lunar exploration vehicles to the moon's surface in soft-landers, to be deployed by a team of earth-bound operators. Both Lunokhods were equipped to carry out a number of scientific experiments, and this technique is considered by experts to be of major importance in the continuing exploration of space. Only by such automatic devices will it be possible to survey planets whose environments are inhospitable to man.

Russia's Salyut 1, launched on 10 April 1971, was also regarded as the first orbital scientific station. The Soyuz 10 spacecraft made an initial $5\frac{1}{2}$-hour docking with it on 24 April, but it was not until 6 June that Soyuz 11 carried cosmonauts Georgi Dobrovolski, Vladislav Volkov and Viktor Patseyev into orbit, to dock with Salyut on the following day. They spent what was then a record of almost 24 days in space, carrying out survey, meteorological, space physics and biological studies, before setting out on the return journey to earth. Tragically, during re-entry their spacecraft suffered decompression, and all of the crew were dead when recovery was effected.

America's Skylab, the proposed launch of which had seemed so many years ahead at the early stages of the Apollo

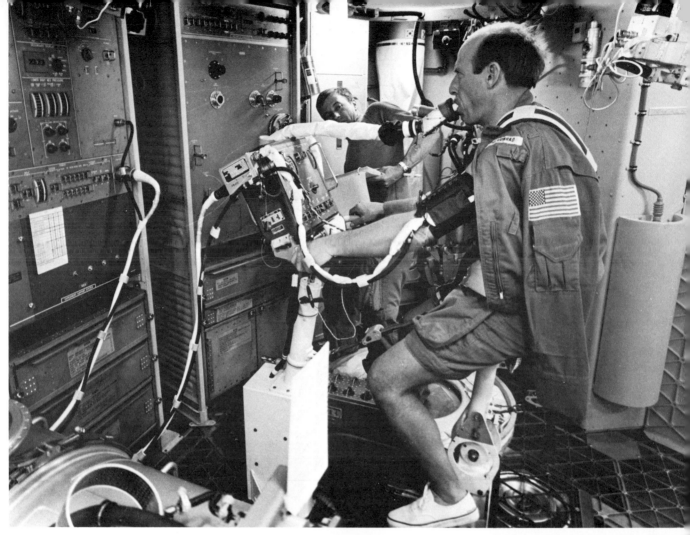

Above: Charles Conrad and Paul J. Weitz, members of the second crew to man America's orbiting space laboratory, check out equipment before Skylab's launch.

Right: The last historic moment of the highly-successful moon-landing programme, as Apollo 17's commander, Eugene A. Cernan, is assisted from the paint-blistered spacecraft floating on the Pacific Ocean.

Far right: Surely the most wonderful view for homeward-bound spaceman is that of Mother Earth, riding serenely and colourfully in the emptiness of space.

Right: The American-Soviet Apollo-Soyuz space mission is planned for 1975. This model shows simulated rendezvous and docking. Not only will such co-operation make it possible to provide rescue for men in distress in space, but it is hoped that it will lead to better understanding between East and West, and lasting peace that will permit time for man's inventive genius to make our world a better place for its ever-growing peoples.

programme, was placed in orbit successfully on 14 May 1973. However, a thin micrometeoroid shield tore loose shortly after lift-off, and it was soon clear that all was not well with the workshop/laboratory/observatory orbiting in space. Power generation capability was down almost 50 per cent because all the solar-cell panels had not deployed, and loss of the micrometeoroid shield, which had the dual task of also providing a thermal shield for the workshop, had caused internal temperatures to soar to a dangerous 190°F (88°C). It seemed that years of work might be wasted.

Special preparations were made so that the first crew of Skylab could make an attempt to salvage the crippled space-station, and it was not until 25 May that they docked their Apollo 'commuter' spacecraft with it. Happily, they succeeded in making Skylab habitable and workable during some strenuous space-walks and completed their 28-day programme of work before splashing down safely in the Pacific on 22 June 1973.

On medical examination the condition of the homecoming crew was found to be satisfactory, and the second three-man team was launched on 28 July, docking successfully. Considerable anxiety was caused, however, by a fuel leak on the Apollo command and service module, and a specially-modified Apollo space capsule was prepared to rescue them. Happily, this was not necessary, and the 59-day mission continued.

Man has already reached out far beyond the moon, using complex scientific space probes to investigate the planets nearest to earth. The probes have already confirmed that Venus has an atmosphere composed almost entirely of carbon dioxide, and that there seems little hope of finding any trace of life—as we know it—on Mars. (This may be confirmed when Russia's Mars 4 and 5, launched on 21 and 25 July 1973 respectively, reach the area of the planet.)

We have not mentioned gliders since the beginning of this history. The omission has been intentional, because by including them here we have come full circle. Their development between the two world wars was considerable, particularly in Germany, which had been forbidden by the Versailles Treaty to build powered aircraft.

Inevitably, during World War II, they were used for military purposes, carrying troops and equipment in some of the epic actions of the war: on Crete, Normandy, Arnhem and New Guinea.

History was to repeat itself in the following years, with Germany again forbidden to build powered aircraft. She developed some of the most advanced examples of what we now more gracefully call 'sailplanes', using new materials and methods of construction to give outstanding performance. Some even have small power plants; but these are to simplify launching and the search for thermals, rather than provide regular powered flight.

In this incredible decade we have also gone back in time, to fly hot-air balloons, a hot-air airship, and to create a 'new' sport of flying hang-gliders, like those which inspired Lilienthal, Pilcher and Chanute.

Who wants a noisy, smelly engine when it is possible to soar like a gull in silent, graceful, purposeful flight? Surely, this has been man's aim from the very beginning—to fly like the birds?

Below: Man is a restless creature, ever seeking new adventures, new challenges. Illustrated is a model of NASA's Viking project. It is hoped to put this odd-looking craft on the surface of the planet Mars in 1976. Before it gets there it will have to travel nearly 460 million miles (740 million km) around the sun.

Right: The NASA/USAF X-24B lifting-body research aircraft built by Martin Marietta.

THE
NEXT
DECADES

*lift the veil of the future
and show us the generations to come*
Walter Rauschenbach

What of the future? Do we really want foresight, or would it merely bring an end to progress? It is, perhaps, the time scale which dominates the answer.

Complicated calculations have foretold that the moon, at present moving away from the earth, will at a point in the future begin to approach again until but it is 11,000 miles (17,703 km) distant. Once it gets as close as this it must inevitably break up as a result of the earth's gravitational pull. What happens then is anybody's guess, but since it is unlikely to occur for about 30,000 million years, why worry? This kind of foreknowledge has no effect on us.

But if the de Havilland Company had been aware that their Comet 1 would end in disaster, could they have carried on with its development? Could we live with a fairly accurate estimate of the date of our deaths?

It is far safer to talk in general rather than in specific terms. For example, not so many years ago when the bugs had just about been eliminated from the TSR.2, well-informed people predicted a great and vital future for this revolutionary tactical strike/reconnaissance aircraft. Who could have forseen its rapid elimination from the scene?

At the time of writing there are, almost certainly, far greater problems for aviation to face than ever before. Few, if any, will deny that technically speaking the Airbus A.300B and BAC/Aérospatiale Concorde are magnificent aircraft. But will it prove possible to sell them in sufficient numbers to make any profit on the enormous capital sum invested in their evolution? It has been suggested that, in the case of the Concorde, the cost involved to date should be written off to research and development. By this means this superb supersonic airliner could be priced realistically and find worthwhile markets.

Can you, at this moment, look out of your window without seeing a single aircraft in the sky? Quite probably you can, yet the airlanes of the world are so crowded that air traffic controllers are becoming numbed with their workload. The pressure does nothing to enhance the high safety factors which research and painstaking work have bestowed upon air travel. Is it inevitable that increasing air traffic must be allied to a reduction in air safety?

In recent years there has, in Britain, been endless talk and comment regarding the pros and cons of a third London airport. Is it really needed? Many will say that it is not. They argue that the pattern of redevelopment of many American airports to accept increased traffic loads should be followed in Britain. But would this now be acceptable to some unfortunate individual who lives beneath the approach or take-off path close to any major airport?

Not surprisingly, the major complaint of those who live near airports is the nerve-shattering noise. How can they be expected to endure this without realistic relief? A munificent supply of double-glazed windows is of little relief on a boiling hot summer evening. As the occupants of such houses twist and turn in their beds in futile attempts to fall asleep, can they be blamed for cursing the names of those

who created the aeroplane?

The much-publicized and predicted 'power crunch' has already arrived. To what extent may this limit air travel? The thought of thirsty aeroplanes like the 'jumbos', which can take on up to 51,000 US gallons (193,051 litres) at a gulp, is a bit staggering. But in terms of passenger miles, this is probably as economic as many motor cars. Yet we are still travelling around on four wheels. The new explosion of war in the Middle East in October 1973 highlighted the gravity of the situation. Reduction of oil supplies from the oil-producing Arab states and escalation in the price of oil has already brought staff lay-offs and service cuts by major airlines. In the search for economy many companies demonstrated that they could achieve very considerable fuel savings by reducing cruising speeds only slightly, and by taxying the big jets on only two engines. If minimal speed increases represent such huge quantities of fuel, what price supersonic transports?

Are there answers to the problems we have posed? Happily, the reply is in the affirmative. To use London's Heathrow Airport as an example, recent figures have shown that passenger traffic has increased by 17 per cent, while aircraft movements are up only two per cent. Such trends are international, and for this we must thank the wide-bodied jets. And there is no doubt that improving technology is making it possible to build engines that create less noise. Thus, logically, the problems of airport capacity, airlane capacity and the sufferings of near-airport dwellers can be reduced by the use of even larger passenger-carrying aircraft, powered by advanced-technology quiet engines.

And since the history of the world suggests that it is unlikely that we can at all times live in peace, one nation with another, is it inevitable that we must continue to create aeroplanes that can kill our fellow men? Sadly, the answer appears to be 'yes' for, although there are signs of improving East-West relationships, there are many other international problems pushing their heads above the surface which may need sterner methods than diplomacy if they are to be solved. The Vietnam war, which flickered and flamed alternately for nearly a decade, is not yet truly over: wisps of smoke still drift in the air. The Middle East war of late 1973 is ended. Disengagement of the combatant nations was very difficult, and there cannot be anyone who believes that any significant move has been made to resolve the antagonism between Arabs and Israelis. But these two conflicts, and the Korean war before them, have shown that wars can be localized. Hopefully, this may be the pattern for the future.

Must we carry our warmongering into space? More recent events suggest this may not be so. The SALT agreement, talks between East and West, and the forthcoming US-Soviet co-operation in an Apollo-Soyuz space mission, all point in the right direction. We may be many, many years away from the generation of the fictional Capt. James Kirk of the starship *Enterprise*, but we would do well to emulate the international peace-keeping role stressed in this television series.

The starship is science fiction today; but it is sobering to put the evolution of aerospace technology into perspective by remembering that there are plenty of people still alive who were born before the Wright brothers made their first flight in a powered heavier-than-air craft. It is quite possible that many who read these lines will have had their doubts that man would ever set foot on the moon!

Left: Vehicles like the X-24B are a step closer to the space shuttle vehicles being developed to carry men to and from space stations in earth orbit, landing conventionally after re-entering earth's atmosphere.

Below: A modern hang-glider for the homebuilder to fly: Icarus II, photographed recently over California. A big pace backward for mankind, to the peaceful days of Chanute, Lilienthal and Pilcher.

INDEX

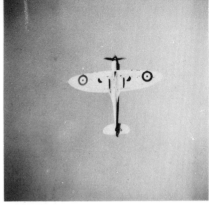

Short quotations in this book are taken from the following publications:
Our Atlantic Attempt by Harry G. Hawker, Methuen & Co Ltd. London, 1919
The Spirit of St. Louis by Charles A. Lindbergh, John Murray (Publishers) Ltd, London, 1953
Wind, Sand and Stars by Antoine de St. Exupéry, Reynal and Hitchcock, New York, 1941
C. W. A. Scott in *Scott's Book*, Hodder and Stoughton, London, 1934
Seaplane Solo by Francis Chichester, Faber and Faber, London, 1932
My Flying Life by Sir Charles Kingsford-Smith, Aviation Book Club, 1939
V2 by W. Dornberger, Hurst and Blackett Ltd., London, 1954
Mathematicall Magick by John Wilkins, Bishop of Chester, 1648
Extract from *US Air Force Magazine*, June 1973

The author and publishers would like to thank those individuals and companies
who have been kind enough to loan the illustrations which have made this book.
Except as detailed below by page number, they come from the collection of
Mr John W. R. Taylor and Mr Michael J. H. Taylor.
They are also grateful to *Personal Plane Services*, High Wycombe, for help with
the jacket photography.

The Aeroplane: pp25 (bottom), 48 (top),
AIR BP: pp26 (bottom), 59 (inset), 100 (top),
Air Portraits: p112,
Camera Press: p37 (bottom),
Flight International: pp34, 39 (bottom), 41 (inset), 46 (bottom), 48 (bottom), 53 (bottom),
Fricke, M: p113 (bottom),
Gilbert, James: pp31 (top), 50 (bottom),
Anne Horton: p6 (below right),
Imperial War Museum: pp37 (top), 36 (bottom), 71 (bottom),
Levy, Howard: pp27, 31 (bottom),
Library of Congress: pp14–15 (top & bottom),
Lufthansa: pp43, 53 (top), 65 (bottom),
McDonough, Kenneth: p50 (top),
McDougall, Harry: p51,
Munson, Kenneth: p98 (top),
NASA: pp22, 23,
Novosti: pp19 (top & bottom), 98 (bottom),
Peckham, Cyril: p49,
Popperfoto: pp6 (bottom left), 20, 38, 39 (top), 52,
Press Association: pp88–9,
Qantas: p18 (top & bottom),
John Rigby: pp2–3, 126, 127, jacket (front & back),
Smithsonian Institution: pp11 (bottom), 13,
USAF: pp11 (top), 21 (bottom), 77, 79,
US Forest Service: p100 (bottom),
Williams, Gordon S: p90

Two RAF Harriers on patrol. With a single flight-refuelling, these remarkable aircraft have a range of more than 3,400 miles (5,472 km).

ACKNOWLEDGMENTS